Praise for *On the Loving End*

Mental illness can shatter even the most loving and secure family. *On the Loving End of Crazy* offers real help for anyone who knows the experience - and it's written by someone who has lived it. Faith Tibbetts McDonald writes from the heart and her compelling story will not only inspire, it will help to heal the broken pieces.
Les Parrott, Ph.D.
New York Times bestselling author of *The Good Fight*

Faith McDonald is generous with her story, and she invites us into her experience in navigating the heartbreaking challenges of a loved one's serious mental illness. She points toward a path for finding help, and her relatable story will offer hope to many.
—Amy Simpson
Author, *Troubled Minds: Mental Illness and the Church's Mission* and *Anxious: Choosing Faith in a World of Worry*

Faith McDonald's *On the Loving End of Crazy* brings an authentic and vulnerable contribution to the mental health conversation. Readers will know they aren't alone and that help and hope do exist for loved ones with mental illness and their care-givers. Faith writes beautifully, bravely, and honestly, and her story will inspire perseverance and faith for families in need of support for mental illness.
--Heather Holleman, speaker and author of *Seated with Christ: Living Freely in a Culture of Comparison* (Moody)

Web address: faithmcdonald.com
Email: faith@faithmcdonald.com

On the Loving End of Crazy

Finding Hope and Help to Face Your Loved One's
Crippling Anxiety and Depression

By
Faith Tibbetts McDonald

On the Loving End of Crazy

To so many of you who have prayed for us and encouraged me in the journey to share our story in book form: You are too many to list; I'd be sure to omit someone. My appreciation is deep and heartfelt. Thank you.

****

This story is nonfiction and told with Matt's permission. Names, except for those of family members, have been changed.

For Matt, with so much love.
Thanks for your willingness to share our story.

Contents

Chapter one: Nightmare

Our family lived a nightmare packed with bizarre twists, thwarted hopes and stark fear. For years, I lived as a casualty in this maze of disaster. Each day, my main task: dread the next crisis. Life's richness faded and other facets of living took place on the outskirts of that main task. I remember every pain.

A doctor said our son Matt might forget—at least, he might forget the worst parts. When people who have lived through similar trauma try to recall their state of mind, they draw blanks. The forgetting is a gift. But my son remembers vivid details leading up to the day, at age twenty-six, his brain betrayed him. He recalls the evening during our spring, Colorado vacation when, with his dad Steve and his brother Phillip, he ate and enjoyed pizza covered in sausage, peppers and cheese. A few hours later, Matt squatted alone in the dark on a rock ledge in the heavy presence of a towering mountain that edges Glenwood Springs, Colorado. He struggled, without success, to silence the voices that urged him to jump.

We aren't sure how far he jumped. He returned from that nighttime walk scratched and bruised, but alive.

When I remember, my muscles clench, and I feel tears collect and grow heavy while they wait for my consent to streak my face with grief. I let them slip, for I have learned that tears are relief. For years, I was so numb I couldn't cry. Each morning when I woke up, I braced to trudge through the day and tried to ignore my pain. I tried to avoid comparing the nonsense of our family's circumstances with the ordered lives of our friends and neighbors. I muddled through.

And now, looking back, I compare the present to my memory of the past and find reasons for gratitude. We survived. As we lived beside Matt, we learned hope. We learned to recognize God's presence in our hardships.

I remember and I find a reason to tell our story. For I think that the valuable lessons I learned and the tools I acquired might equip you to find your way through similar darkness with more agility, maybe, more efficiently, and with less pain. For there is a way through. People with mental illness can get better. That's the happy end to my story and I want it to be the happy end to your story.

But first let me tell you about the pain-filled middle of our story.

Matt wrote down his memories of eating pizza and squatting alone on that mountainside. He let me read his account a few months after our vacation in Colorado which included him lunging from a moving car as it wound through the Vail Pass. He opened the backseat passenger door, plunged to the asphalt, rolled, righted himself and ran off the road, trudging into deep snow that slowed him.

Steve was driving, and immediately, he pulled the car to the road's shoulder and jumped out to chase Matt. As Phillip watched, bewildered, Steve caught up with Matt, pushed him down into the snow and, so he'd agree to return to the warmth of the car, wrestled his coat and shirt off.

Matt resisted vehemently.

Just off the shoulder of a heavily traveled highway, two members of my family rolled and pulled and yelled. One man pinned another down and stripped him of clothes on a frigid, windy day. Cars whizzed by. No one slowed or stopped to help.

Months passed before Matt explained his actions. He fled, he said, because he thought Steve and Phillip were plotting to harm him. He felt compelled to find a place to hole up surrounded by trees in the snowy Colorado wilderness. He wanted to die there. As the thoughts of fear and flight ticked through his mind, he knew they were nonsense, yet he lacked the power to stop them.

Here's an excerpt from his written story:

> That winter my family took a ski trip out to the Colorado Rocky Mountains. The skiing was really good, but my depression and anxiety set in. On the way up the ski lift I had thoughts of suicide. These thoughts were not new. At home, I had thought many times, "I should shoot myself."
>
> While skiing, I didn't want to think of suicide. I had planned to ski and have fun. But I thought things like, "I should jump off the lift. Or when I get to the top, I should ski off the back of the mountain."
>
> However, I didn't do it and when I didn't, I thought, "I'm a failure because I can't. Am I too scared?"
>
> We skied two more days and then I stayed at the condo the fourth day because I was feeling bad and depressed and I couldn't enjoy myself. On our last night in Glenwood Springs my anxious thoughts finally got to me and I cracked. I got up out of bed, put my clothes on, took my suitcase which was already packed, and left the house with intentions of killing myself. I walked the streets of the small town, rolling my suitcase behind me. I came to a dumpster. I thought, "Well, I won't be needing this." And I put my suitcase in it.

After reading, I ask, "Why didn't you tell us? Then?"

On vacation, we'd noticed his sullen silence. He kept going off to ski by himself; we didn't know why and when we invited him to stay with us, he got prickly.

Months later, when he explained, he said, "Nobody wants to ruin a vacation by saying, 'I'm thinking of killing myself.'"

And I think: so you try to complete the act instead? Like that wouldn't ruin a vacation? But I push my lips tightly together.

I don't want to say anything that will deter him from sharing his story. I want him to keep talking.

Before the Colorado vacation, for a few long years, eight to be exact, he'd been sullen and silent. I'd rifle my brain to come up with ways to get him to talk. Often, I bargained with him. "I'll massage your shoulders, if you'll tell me about your day."

He'd say, "Massage my scalp."

I rubbed his head, and in return, he'd say, tops, two three-word sentences.

"You are so stingy with your words," I'd complain. He'd shrug and go off to take a nap.

Family members stood on the sidelines of his stalled, miserable life. We watched, waited and fervently hoped and prayed for the return of the loving, enthusiastic person we'd once known; we prayed that Matt would thrive. Like I mentioned, this book is the story of those hopes eventually met and God's answer to our prayers. I'm telling this story because I want to encourage you as you wait for your hopes to be met and for a glimmer of a sign that God hears your prayers.

Plus, my therapist says I need to talk. "There are so many things you haven't processed."

When she says this, I remind myself that I am in that room, sitting on that couch, talking to her because I want to be. I've chosen to be there. I remind myself, because, honestly, her comment irks me. I consider myself an A student. (These days, I'm a teacher, not a student. But I still measure work quality in A's and B's.) I do not leave tasks undone.

And process? What does that even mean? It takes me a week, but at our next session I ask her.

I don't recall her answer word for word. But it seems to me that processing is identifying memories that still spark fear or sadness or despair or anger and describing them in words. This act can prompt a new perspective and can keep the memories from developing a life of their own that haunts me with fear, sadness, despair or anger that looms large and is more detrimental to healthy living than the events that prompted the memories.

The untangling includes remembering an event, talking about the feelings it evoked and figuring out how to dismantle its power. Processing is not easy. Sometimes it gives me a headache. I wonder if maybe some events and feelings can't be processed because they just sucked.

Here's an example of an event that scared and confused me. During those long years, we lived through plenty of them. We were often bewildered and worried by inexplicable things Matt said and did. Recalling this one still makes me shake inside.

One hot summer evening, I sat next to twenty-three-year-old Matt on our front porch steps. He wasn't feeling well. He'd come home early from his job at a carwash because, he reported, the people at work acted as if they didn't like him.

Steve mowed our lawn with a push mower. I inhaled the smell of cut grass and felt the lawnmower's purr rattle through me. I noticed the grass clumps strewn in the mower's swath. They'd get damp overnight and be tracked into the house In the morning. Someone should rake. I recalled clumsy dusk-time cartwheels I'd attempted on the summer lawns of my childhood. I felt sad that Matt thought the people at work didn't like him.

"Have you grouched at them?" I asked. Maybe they reacted to his gloomy, gruff aloofness which stemmed from extreme depression and anxiety.

Steve pushed the mower to cut a swath of grass close to our gravel driveway. He was too close. The mower blade met rocks. It crunched loudly, gurgled and spat a handful of pebbles.

Matt lurched, and jumped up from his seat on the step, agitated. "You see that? I think Dad wants to murder me."

"What?"

I hopped to my feet, put my hand on his arm, and looked up into his eyes. He shifted to evade my gaze. "I think Dad—

and you—want to murder me."

I have heard the occasional story of parents who murder their kids. This is not one of those stories. We are not those kind of parents. I have heard a parent growl to a son or daughter, "I'm going to kill you if you do that again." I have heard kids say things like, "My mom will kill me if I..." and then they mention an undesirable action like fail a test or get a speeding ticket or text while driving.

I've probably, okay have, threatened to kill a kid who pushed his curfew or neglected to clean up a spill in the refrigerator. But, of course, the voiced threat never actually meant violence. I meant kill as a hyperbole for I'm-annoyed-with-you. I wanted to express irritation with vehemence. But I didn't mean murder.

I may be naïve, but I have never even met a parent who was an actual danger to his or her children. I imagine murderous parents are angry, substance-induced stupid, and hostile. We are grateful, alert, and loving.

Like you, we are the kind of parents who protected our kids. We arranged our schedules to accommodate our kids. If we couldn't be there for them, we arranged for a vetted caretaker. And the vetting process we employed was extensive. Similar to a TSA agent's pre-boarding security check of a sketchy-looking wannabe airline passenger.

Like you, we are the parents who smile wide at our kids' smiles and forfeit sleep to toss and turn when our kids feel wretched because, say, they didn't make the varsity basketball team. Or when they feel miffed because, say, they wanted to upgrade their cell phone, but we refused to spend the money.

We look out for our kids' health. They had regular checkups, vaccinations and healthy food. I made Matt's baby food from organic vegetables before organic was a thing. I'm the mom who took infant CPR classes just in case. After my babies' baths, I patted their soft skin dry with a downy towel and scrutinized their healthy chests to locate the described spot for two finger rapid compressions. I wondered if I should mark the spot with a black permanent marker heart just in case a catastrophe smote me too panicked to locate it.

We are present for our kids. We attended their events, whether educational, sporting or music lesson related. After long days at work, we gulped meat pulled from a grocery store rotisserie chicken, carrot sticks and some cold mac and cheese, so we could hurry to back-to-school night, where we perched in little chairs and listened intently to teachers explain curriculum expectations and no-bullying rules and the fact that one of the school's 450 students was so highly allergic to peanuts that every student was asked to go without peanut butter sandwiches for lunch. All year long.

We promoted their interests. We are the parents who got our kids pets and long after the kids' pet interest waned, we fed and watered and walked those pets.

We are the kind of parents who did homework with our kids, took them to church and youth group, who went without things, so our kids could have the things they need. Or just wanted.

I am not trying to convince you that I deserve a parenting award, or even a pat on the back. I just want you to know, for certain, that I am not the kind of mother that knowingly or willingly hurts her kid.

Matt knew that the day he blurted his panicked, "I think you and Dad want to murder me." He had lived with us for more than twenty years. How could he be so bizarrely confused?

"Why do you think that Dad and I want to harm you?" I asked.

"You see what he did with those stones?"

You think Dad's going to murder you with pebbles? Using the lawn mower blade to launch them? That sounds, well, far-fetched.

This can't be about us. It must be you. Do you have unresolved guilt? Prompting bizarre thoughts? We've disagreed more often than not over the past few years—sometimes heatedly—do you feel guilty about that?

I didn't voice my thoughts. But I thought about the stress that had built up between Steve, Matt, and me.

During Matt's senior year of high school, his partying had included alcohol and other illegal substances. For a while, he partied and functioned reasonably, but eventually circumstances spiraled downward for him. He managed to land part-time jobs but was repeatedly fired. He entered and then dropped out of college. He was arrested for behavior tied to unhealthy binge drinking—more than a few times. The havoc stressed our family. Steve and I tried to respond to the chaos with love, but we'd argued with Matt, and each other, a lot.

Do you think we want to hurt you because we've yelled at you? Do you think we want to hurt you because you've hurt us? We forgive you; you know. Dad and I. We love you.

I didn't explain my immense bewilderment to Matt. I thought my confusion might increase his unsettledness. I stressed that I loved him and suggested he take a nap while I made dinner.

I felt so disconcerted inside. Like I felt when I was a kid in the fun house of an amusement park where I flung myself on a spinning disk that spun faster and faster until my grip was loosed and I rolled off into the floor, collapsed and dizzy. The summer day when Matt said he thought we wanted to murder him, I felt physically and emotionally bewildered. I tried to find my bearings so I could move to life's next task, but my thoughts and emotions swirled. Matt's behavior did not make sense. I did not know what to do.

I hoped, because I didn't know any better, Matt would nap in his upstairs bedroom and, maybe, wake from this nonsensical nightmare that included me.

A few moments later, he barreled down the stairs. I tried to lay my hand on his arm. To calm him. To remind him of our loving connection. To evade interaction with me, he darted and weaved his way to a shelf. He grabbed his wallet and car keys. He ran out the door to his car, started it and erupted out of the driveway. Stones flew.

Steve stopped mowing, threw his hands up in frustration and hollered after Matt, "Slow down!"

I wondered how to tell Steve that the son we adored fled because he thought we wanted to murder him.

Matt was missing for two days.

Missing, physically, that is. The Matt I knew, the Matt I'd

birthed, the essence of the son we'd raised and loved for two decades was missing for much longer. The length of his illness was due in part to our cluelessness. We had no idea what we were facing and we had no idea how to get the help we desperately needed.

Sometimes, I still feel angry and stupid about that. It is a regret that needles me, and the needle is big and sharp and hot. We didn't know how much he needed help. And we are educated people, but we didn't know where to begin to get help.

How's that for processing?

Please don't stop reading thinking that this story will be too sad to bear, because eventually we learned how much Matt needed help and he got it. I don't want to give away the ending, but this is a story of hope. This is the story of getting Matt back. I'm telling you this story because I hope it will help you endure the hard times and give you tools to use to navigate the confusing maze of loving someone through severe anxiety, depression, or another kind of mental illness.

When we flailed in the pain of thick despair, no one told us that Matt could get better. When I mention to mental health practitioners that life would have been easier had they said he could get better, they say that there's no knowing.

I am so grateful for the experienced nurse who confidently assured me of hope. "Matt will get better. I've seen people get better from worse than this."

I want you to hear a resounding declaration of the possibility—the potential—for your loved one to get better. So this is a story of healing and hope when healing seems distant and hope seems, well, foolish.

This is a story about what to do when life is so ruined there's nothing you can do. This is a story about a mom (me) who prays desperately, day after day, into the vast silence. Who sometimes feels that while she calls her words prayers, they are only a frantic form of worry. Sometimes it seems like circumstances are choppy, turbulent waves, she is drowning, and her prayers are fading flails for help. In God's time, which seems like a long time, he answers. And processing his answer is a sacred meditation fueled by gratitude.

But before I tell you that part, I'd like to tell you a little about Matt. If you get to know Matt, you will love him and appreciate his story. If you know him, you will cheer for him and long for him to emerge a hero when he seems to be the villain working tirelessly to destroy his own life.

Chapter two: Matt and Me

"I didn't really want to commit suicide; I have always had a zest for life and enjoyed the simple things. The thoughts were just overbearing and made my head ache."

When I read Matt's written words describing his confusion, I wished he had voiced his turmoil when he felt it, so that we could have helped. And I worried that if he had voiced his thoughts, their significance would have eluded me.

Usually, I worry excessively about insignificant things. I can fret a freckle into melanoma at warp speed. While I'm flossing, I can stew a lull in a late-night text exchange with my daughter who lives in Haiti into her kidnapping by criminals who demand a hefty ransom. However, once in a great while, I misread a situation and choose nonchalance when urgency is called for.

Once, a few years ago, Steve came home from playing pick-up basketball feeling uneasy. "I feel strange. In the middle of the game, I got dizzy and then I lost my vision for about a minute."

"Happens to me all the time," I said with a dismissive wave of my hand meant to diminish his concern. I have never played pick-up basketball. I meant the dizzy feeling. "Why don't you take a nap? And eat a sandwich. Yeah, eat a sandwich. Your blood sugar's probably low."

A few days later, almost past the lifesaving window of opportunity, a neurologist showed me pictures of Steve's torn carotid artery and mentioned the life-threatening possibility of a blood clot catching on the flap. Urgency and a panicked oops swelled within me. I didn't offer the neurologist a sandwich.

Imagine Matt saying, "Mom, I'm thinking of k-wording myself." (These days, I like to skirt the word kill. Especially when my kids are involved. The word brings back waves of those unprocessed memories.) Caught off-guard by his admission, I might have flapped my hand breezily and said something ineptly casual like, "Happens to me all the time. Why don't you help me by flipping these grilled cheese sandwiches? And it's your turn to take out the garbage."

Or I might have scolded him. "Stop talking like that. We don't k-word people. Not even ourselves." As silly as that sounds, I admit that I thought for years that acts like suicide didn't happen in my sphere. Suicide, I thought, if I thought of it at all, is the desperate act of derelict others.

I probably would have scolded.

So even though we are not the type of family that is rearranged by suicide—or so I thought—suicide invaded Matt's thoughts. Curiously, trapped in chaotic, overwhelming thoughts of self-destruction, he wielded apt self-awareness. He recognized that for most of his life, he had exuded zest for life and joy. It didn't take much—a family bike ride, a puppy romping over him, a friend coming by to watch basketball and shoot hoops in the driveway, a tasty meal—to prompt his grin.

He was a happy kid.

Evidence of his happiness, his grin, practically bounces from a snapshot that's tacked to a bulletin board on the wall in the hallway to our basement. In the picture, Matt is smiling wide and flanked by two high school friends. During the dark days of Matt's lengthy depression, leading up to the Colorado trip, I'd pause on a trip down the stairs to the laundry room to look at the picture and ache and plead, "God, please return his smile."

I'm perplexed that I didn't record the date of his first smile on the Baby's First Year Calendar on which I detailed his milestones. I have other firsts recorded. The first day he held his head up. His first Valentine's Day and the cards he received. A few days later, his first vaccination. On vaccination day, the notation says: Matt has a temp of 103 degrees. Mama wonders if he'll smile again. The next day: Even with a temperature of 101 degrees, Matt smiles at Mom.

I wrote those phrases, tuned to his smiles, unaware that the time would come when I'd trudge through dark months which would turn to years, while I wondered: will he ever smile again? Sometimes, during the dark years I'd think, I don't recognize my own child. Of course, I recognized his physical features, but I didn't recognize the bulky, ominous, speechless gloom that trailed him and emanated from him like a foul fume.

When I picture young adult Matt, crouching in the gloom of a Colorado mountain's shadow, trudging dimly lit streets, and eventually depositing his suitcase in a dumpster, I flinch and puzzle about how he got to that bizarre state of mind. Am I to blame? Should I have controlled his life more? Or differently?

God gave Steve and me a perfect little boy and while I was nervous about first-time parenting, I set out to make him more perfect. Matt was born on December 4, 1986. He weighed about seven-and-a-half pounds and was twenty-one inches or so long. He had ten fingers. Ten toes. I counted them all. Many times. He had a cute little pug nose and two exquisitely ridged ears that fit nicely against the sides of his head and worked well. As a former teacher for hearing-impaired children, I felt compelled to test my baby's hearing by clapping and observing his reaction. His tiny startled response convinced me that he heard the claps.

A couple of days after he'd been born, as I sat on the edge of the hospital bed, waiting for Steve to pick us up, I wrapped my arms around my swaddled baby and held him close. I felt huge qualms. The newness of all the parenting tasks and responsibilities overwhelmed me. I wanted to do everything right, and I worried that I wouldn't. I countered the doubts with a stern pep talk. Sixteen-year-old girls take babies home from the hospital. You are twenty-nine, well-educated and an experienced teacher to boot. You've got this covered.

I wanted to control our lives so that he got more perfect, was always happy, and (I'm only admitting this to you-- please don't spread it around.) people admired me for being such an accomplished mother. By the time our third child arrived, I'd relaxed and just wanted to sit and hold her and be grateful for her—a far easier way to parent. In contrast, the parents Matt knew us as might have been, okay, were tense, and a little frantic. I can't speak for Steve, but although I was nervous about parenting, I was also a little too impressed with the ability I thought I possessed to control life, so it would turn out as I pleased.

As a novice parent, I wanted my children to perform flawlessly in a quaint paradise that I constructed by barring bad influences and dousing my children with love, education, protectiveness and positive vibes. Go ahead. Shake your head. I'm shaking mine. Had I exchanged some important brain parts for cotton candy?

I sure didn't foresee how haphazardly, recklessly and close to home my children would collide with life's downside. I didn't realize how disease, and the children's choices— some of them foolish, some of them just not mine—would take their paths out of my control. I wanted to control their environment. And them. Just a little, okay, a lot. For their own good.

Early, I learned that my control would be contested in small things. I recall pushing baby Matt in a stroller on the country road we lived on just after a rainstorm. A truck came rolling down the gravel road and splashed us, splattering Matt in cold, muddy water. He cried.

"Slow down!" I hollered and shook my fist in the air. Drivers on the hill that crested in front of our home should show regard for my treasure.

Our neighbor, a grandfather, noting my dismay, pointed out gruffly, "It may be the first time that baby's covered in mud, but it won't be the last."

I heard him. But I didn't buy in. I thought I could eliminate Matt's interactions with life's messes and muck.

Matt was a chatty little kid. I valued our conversations. I remember the first time Matt talked about life after death and realized we don't take things with us. My grandmother had passed away and my dad flew from his home in Connecticut to her home in Vancouver, British Columbia to tend to her estate. Six weeks later, arrangements complete, Dad was on his way home to Connecticut by car and he planned to stay overnight with us in Pennsylvania.

"Grandpa's coming. He won't be driving his car. He'll be driving Great Grandma's car. It's white." I explained to Matt who watched for his grandfather to pull in the driveway.

"Why's Grandpa driving Great Grandma's car?" Cars matter to Matt.

"Grandma wrote in her will that Grandpa could have her car when she died."

"Why didn't she take it to heaven with her?"

For a quiet moment, I considered an explanation appropriate for a six-year-old. Matt beat me to one. "I guess she couldn't take it to heaven because it would fall through the clouds."

I guess so.

I guess that's why he put the suitcase in the dumpster. He didn't want his stuff from life here to fall through the clouds.

I don't know about you, but I don't spend a lot of time wondering what life after life here is like. I believe it will be good. I'll exchange pain for joy. I want to be there with God and Jesus and friends who've preceded me.

I want my kids to be there, too. To ensure that they are headed heavenward, sometimes, I tried to manipulate their interactions with almighty God. Like God couldn't be trusted with that. Or them.

I remember quizzing Matt on his spiritual state. At six-years-old, or so, Matt reassured me. "Yup. Jesus lives in my heart." He looked down at his chest, pulled on the hem of his t-shirt and scrutinized the stretched surface. As a kid who took things literally, maybe he looked for a door to the inside.

"What's Jesus doing in there?" I asked. I'd wondered what he thought.

"Making breakfast."

I just so much wanted him to believe—to be on the right track for his time here and for ever after.

When he was in fifth grade, his school class toured the Columbus chapel at the Boalsburg mansion in Boalsburg, Pennsylvania. The tour guide displayed a variety of antique treasures, including large splinters of wood and claimed, "These are pieces of wood from Christ's cross."

Ten-year-old Matt was impressed. "If they have pieces from the real cross, the bible must be true."

I wanted him to believe, but I didn't want him to be swindled into belief. In the spirit of full disclosure, I reminded him that wood rots and he'd seen evidence of that in the woods near our home. "Do you think those are really pieces of Jesus' cross?" I asked, pressing him to think deeper.

Parenting so my kids would pursue faith and go to heaven for life eternal was high on my list of priorities. I wanted it to be real faith, prompted by sound reasons.

As a young parent, I learned that my sway would be upended by circumstances and wrested from me by the children themselves as they grew to be individuals. Matt seized control when he could.

As soon as he could climb out of his crib, he got up earlier than I wanted every morning. He'd bounce down the stairs, "Mommy. Sun's up. I'm up."

He was a particular eater. Once he started eating solid food, he insisted that it be the same color as Steve's and mine. If our plates held corn, chicken and French fries, Matt wanted yellow mush, white mush and a real fry set out on his highchair tray.

Even as a young child, Matt did not embrace change easily. When seasons changed, he put off adjusting his clothing as long as possible. One fall, he wore his favorite summer garb: a short sleeve white t-shirt, mustard-colored gym shorts and black, rubber barn boots—until snow fell.

Another year, he outgrew his favorite pair of footie pajamas. He pulled them on and discovered that wearing them required slight awkward knee bends. I explained that I would cut off the pajama feet and he could wear the pajamas without contortions. But my explanation must have been unclear because when I offered him the pajamas with the feet cut off, he wailed.

Before his first week of kindergarten, I explained my plan to drive him to school for the first week and said that when he grew accustomed to school, he could take the school bus. He asked what the other kids do. I explained that I didn't know. Privately, I thought that the other mothers might not be as motivated to ensure their child's gradual and positive adjustment to school. He said, "I think I'd like to take the bus on the first day and from then on." And he did. The first morning, he shouldered his backpack, climbed the school bus steps on his sturdy little legs, turned, grinned and waved.

For the most part he liked the bus ride. One day he confided in alarm that one of the little girls he sat next to on the bus had said the s-word to him.

"The s-word? What's that?"

"Shut-up," he whispered in my ear. He was our first child and we filtered life and language for him. By the time our third came along, I'm sure her brothers had taught her the s-word and more before she was two.

Matt loved his brother and sister and was always looking out for them.

Once, Carolyn, who is six years younger than he is, handed him a doll to play with. For a moment he gingerly held it at arm's length, looking it over. "You could be the doctor," I suggested.

"I'm the daddy." He resolved and draped the baby doll over his shoulder and gently patted her back.

With Phillip, he'd play rougher, more active games. One time, I went to the back door to see him struggling to carry Phillip across the lawn. The boys had been practicing jumps and other tricks on their bikes. Phillip had crashed and hit his head on concrete. Blood ran down the side of his head.

After the hurried trip to the emergency room for stitches and advice on how to care for a young boy with a concussion, at home, I asked Matt, "What did Phillip think when you picked him up?"

"He didn't know. He was sleeping." He'd been knocked

out cold. At this news, my alarm at the severity of Phillip's fall ratcheted up a notch.

When Matt was seven and in second grade, we moved from the small town in Northwestern Pennsylvania where I had thought we'd live for the rest of our lives to a larger town in Central Pennsylvania. In that year's school picture, Matt's enormous brown eyes seep with sadness. The move might have been his first real brush with life change. It was difficult for him. I sometimes wondered if that move was the unsettling circumstance that set him on the path to despair. But I have since learned that anxiety disorder and clinical depression are diseases. The change in residence did not cause the mental health issues that Matt eventually faced.

I recall the first time anxiety interfered with Matt's life. I didn't recognize the occurrence as outside the scope of normal. But now, I wonder. Should I have recognized the red flag?

Here's what happened. In 1992, we lived about thirty miles from the city of Erie where, tragically, a little girl was kidnapped, murdered and left in a dumpster by an unknown perpetrator. The search for the villain was massive. Broadcast television and radio updates blared regularly. The crime and chase filled the local paper.

I did not mention the situation to my kids. By then, we had two: Matthew and Phillip. Steve and I discreetly discussed the tragedy. Behind closed doors and covered mouths, we assured each other that the vile creep wasn't a danger to us. We lived way out in the country. But we agreed that a little hypervigilance might be called for. I upped the fervor with which I watched our kids. I made sure I knew where they were at all times. When they played outside, I asked them to report in often.

Right around that time, Matt woke up one night, writhing and complaining that his stomach hurt. He couldn't fall back to sleep. So we couldn't fall back to sleep. In the morning, I took him to the doctor, who checked him all over, but did not determine a cause for the pain.

During the day, Matt recovered. The next night, he woke crying and contorting in pain. The pattern continued. We took a trip to the emergency room to rule out appendicitis. Days later, the doctor ordered some exploratory tests.

We were so worried. Our young son was surrounded by hard, metal instruments and task-oriented medical professionals who inserted a scope into his rectum to determine the cause of his ailment. We cringed that he had to endure the procedure but identifying the cause of his pain was necessary. And, elusive. The procedure did not reveal a medical cause for his discomfort, and the doctor resorted to prescribing medicine for anxiety.

I didn't connect the dots. I wondered what caused his anxiety. But did I ask him?

Eventually, the little girl's murderer was captured, and his mug shot featured on the front page of the paper. Six-year-old Matt picked the paper up and held up the picture. "Is that the man who kidnapped and killed that little girl?" he asked.

"Yes, but how do you know about him?"

"I've heard about him on the news. I know you read about him in the paper."

A few days later, Matt revealed the extent of his worry while playing with his cousin Alexandra. They sat on top of our long chest freezer, sorting building blocks. They'd decided to play up high, away from their three-year-old siblings who didn't treat their Lego creations with care.

I overheard them talking about what they were going to make. Alexandra said that she planned to make a house.

"I am going to make a house, too. And I am going to put a very high fence around it, as high as the house, so that bad guys like the kidnapper can't ever get in," said Matt. And then he reported to his cousin, in vivid detail, the story of the crime.

Everything in me screamed, "Protect! Protect more." I wish I had seized the opportunity to teach Matt ways to deal with acute anxiety. I wish that, while assuring Matt that as his parents, we would do our best to keep him safe, I had focused on helping him learn techniques for dealing with anxiety.

I was all about protecting, but now I know that I did not clearly understand the kind of protection my son needed. I thought I needed to protect him from outside harm. I didn't know mental illnesses like anxiety disorders and major depression can settle in and become so powerful that they seize control of people's brains.

What if we had gotten him help for coping with anxiety after that first incident?

Some days, when young adult Matt was stalled in the ruin of depression and self-destructive behavior, I wondered how I'd failed. Was my control too lax? Or did I try to exert too much?

What if I had parented differently? Maybe you recognize that question. Maybe, like me, as you watch your loved one struggle, you find you are very good at second guessing, at going through the past and identifying places where you could have, or should have, acted differently. For years, I returned to those places again and again and again. But I have learned to let that practice go. We don't get to send our wiser, savvy selves back to redo the past. We just get to move on from the present. The best thing we can do if we can't get out of the what-if mire is find a good counselor and process. Not easy, I know. But worth it.

Chapter three: A Prayer

Fast forward to spring 2005. Matt is eighteen and about to graduate from high school.

The evening before the graduation ceremony, I sat on the edge of my seat in a church auditorium for a baccalaureate ceremony. I couldn't settle in. For years, I'd been focused on orchestrating a life for that kid, our graduate-to-be. Highschool graduation was one of the milestones I'd anticipated celebrating. I wasn't sure this weekend was going to go according to plan.

Matt had balked when I announced our family's plans to attend the baccalaureate service. His reaction stirred my fears that he was choosing a life that veered from the one I had in mind for him.

He didn't want to attend the service which was hosted by Christian teachers who taught at our local high school. The purpose of the service was to add a spiritual perspective to the graduation celebration and acknowledge the God who gave the gifts of intelligence and education and ask his blessing and presence in the graduates' lives and futures.

It wasn't a secret gathering. But it wasn't an official function promoted by our town's public school.

"It's optional. I don't have to go," Matt had said.

I disagreed. I wanted us to go. "Your friends will be there," I coaxed.

He conceded with a slight nod. Then countered. "I have friends who won't be there, too. I'd rather be with them."

Those other friends. Probably the reason he'd grown to

dislike church, neglect school and tried to dodge family time and interactions. He wanted to shed us, so he could be more like them.

"We need to support activities like this service and the teachers who organize them."

"I don't."

Even so, I'd summoned the energy, the force, to ensure that our graduate and every member of our family showed up for the baccalaureate and was dressed appropriately. I'm intent on promoting family togetherness. We should all celebrate each other's achievements.

In the auditorium, we waited for the service to start. The graduates, dressed in caps and gowns, sat together in the first few rows. I scanned the back of their heads, looking for my son. It was hard to see his neck and shoulders. He's tall, about six-foot-one, but at that stage of life, and in church, he tended to slouch and sit arms crossed, his arms a barricade.

Matt wore the maroon graduation gown and cap that matched his peers'. At my urging he'd picked up the attire in the nick of time. His thick, dirty-blond, shoulder-length hair was combed and pulled back into a ponytail that some gorgeous, older girl who was on track to be a sports reporter had called sexy. The small, gold cross that pierced his ear was probably visible. At least it was a Christian symbol. I had developed a habit of mitigating my dismay by measuring Matt's appearance and actions against dire could-have-beens. The earring could have been two earrings and they could have been skull and crossbones. Or he could have marked himself with a permanent, colorful tattoo mural that depicted and broadcasted the rebel life philosophy he was trying out.

I imagined the scowl that twisted his face. It seemed more-or-less permanent. His hair, his earring, his grimace, and the hostility he exuded—normal expressions of adolescent push-back, right?

Or was he imploding? I often felt vaguely afraid. That things weren't going as planned and that was not okay. Life's supposed to be okay.

However, our whole family present in the auditorium for

the ceremony signified a mission accomplished. Our oldest child was through high school and on his way to college. I waited for that we're-all-in-church-together glow to engulf me.

But were we present on false pretenses? I started to worry. Was he really going to graduate? I'd been on the phone with the guidance counselor multiple times during the last few months of Matt's senior year. The counselor attributed Matt's behavior to senioritis. I had heard of senioritis, but I didn't think it was a real thing. I had graduated in the top ten percent of my class, and thought, now, I realize, so naively, that the world was divided into two groups of people: us—people who aspired to high academic standing—and them—people who dropped out of life. For about the last year, Matt had aligned himself with "them". He'd spent the semester repeatedly skipping school, skimping on studying and failing many tests. There were two classes he might not pass. I found Matt's actions bewildering.

The school counselor said, "I think Matt knows just what he needs to do to get by and that's what he's doing. He'll graduate."

Bare minimum. But our family doesn't do bare minimum in school. I'm a teacher. My kids love school. We value education. But when I saw Matt's English teacher in the grocery store, I avoided her. I didn't recognize Matt's approach to school. I didn't recognize his attitude and I sure didn't want to try and explain it.

When Matt was in kindergarten, he'd attended a small school where they held quaint kindergarten graduation ceremonies. Each student wore a miniature white cap and gown. As a smiling six-year-old, Matt wore his white cap and gown as if he'd been equipped to float joyfully in air. During the commencement ceremony, the class sang a song. Matt smiled so widely, sang so enthusiastically that exuberance seemed to burst out of him like he was a piece of popped corn. His body the kernel and joy the white cloud.

Twelve years later, hostility had become his mainstay.

I glanced around the church sanctuary which was filled

with graduates' family members. I knew most of them. I wondered if any other graduates were barely eking out a diploma.

I worried. What happened to people who didn't graduate? Who didn't complete this life ritual on time? My son would mature back into animated joy, right? I feared there was a ledge and people who didn't graduate on time tumbled over the edge into ruin.

I hoped my fears were exaggerated.

But I couldn't spend too much time hoping. I had to steer my family through the rituals of graduation. We had to maneuver this rite of passage. I wished we could do it happily. It was supposed to be a happy, normal achievement. Why did I have to force him through this gate? Had I purchased my share of the food we'd need for the graduation party Matt would share with his cousin Alexandra? Chips, check. Soda, check. Cake. Had I said I'd get balloons?

The speaker, a Christian gym teacher, moved to the front of the room. I whispered to my husband. "Remember that teacher? Matt had him for gym. Matt liked him. Maybe Matt will listen to what he says."

I often tried to conjure up the bright side of our circumstances and fling it—a large protective covering—to envelop Steve.

The speaker began. He spoke about a prayer from Ephesians 3:17-20. He challenged participants to let God help them identify a specific individual and to pray the prayer for that individual for thirty days in a row. His spiel sounded a little like a prosperity gospel message. If you do such and such, God will do for you beyond your wildest dreams.

I don't put much stock in these systems that humans invent to describe how God works. And, at that time, I was in a bit of a crisis of faith regarding God's promises. I'd been in a bible study that year where we discussed a verse that said something like, "Raise up a child in the way he should go and when he is grown, he will not depart from it." I think it's in Proverbs.

"That's not a promise," one woman said.

"What?" every fear in me amped up to high alert. "That's a promise I was banking on. What do you mean it's not a promise?" Those words are scripture. Written how many thousand years ago? On a scroll and then accepted as God's word by the wise men on the council of Nicaea.

"It's not a promise. It's a statement of how things are intended to work, but God doesn't promise that's how it will always work."

I tried to shake off her dour perspective. But her words had injected me with doubt.

I liked the baccalaureate speaker's take better. I liked the idea that there might be something I could do to procure a large share of God's attention for my kid. I determined to pray the prayer for Matt, and I made up my mind to pray it until I knew it was answered.

The act gave me something to do in my desperation.

I began to pray diligently. Every day, I read and prayed the verses in Ephesians 3:17-20. I prayed that God who is wealthy in all Matt needed and desired would live in Matt and that Matt would be engulfed by God's wide, high, long love and that Matt would be filled with the fullness of God.

So that my prayers would not be rote and repetitive, I personalized them in my journal. "Today, God, my son seems stuck in ruin, hopelessness and despair. He exudes hostility. Help him turn to you. You are so rich in all the good things we need to live fulfilling lives. You desire to share, if we come to you and ask. So today, I ask for my son. Let him turn to you for the rich meaning life requires. Dismantle his apathy for you. Let him see the good things you have for him: satisfaction, power to live, company with your good spirit. Thrill him with the knowledge that you, the Creator, love him more thoroughly, more exuberantly than he could ever imagine. I trust you, the only one who can work in his life more powerfully than I can ask or imagine."

Each day, I wrote the prayer a little differently, but the themes were the same. "Give my son strength to live. Keep him company deep in his spirit. Overwhelm him with love."

After barely graduating, Matt continued to live outside the lines of what I thought was normal or wise. A great dismalness coated his features and seemed to gnaw at him. It separated him from family, from desire to succeed in school or pursue other options.

He determined to attend college because that's what his friends were doing. Because I worked at the university, his tuition was discounted. The discount was supposed to be a blessing, but without it, he couldn't have gone to college and maybe then he'd have sought out a different pathway instead of a conveyor belt to disaster.

In the fall of 2005, he moved into an on-campus dorm, even though the university he attended was only a few miles from home. He kept us at arm's length, only contacting us when he wanted to borrow the car.

Occasionally, he looked me up for help with his English papers. He was taking a course I had taught many times. His writing process made me cringe. His keyboarding skills were ragged. His writing had potential. But he did all his work at the last minute. His habits were the habits of students who failed. As much as I longed for him to succeed, I knew the work habits he practiced couldn't be rewarded in the long run.

Thanksgiving came. It was our Thanksgiving to meet with my extended family in the Poconos. I wasn't sure Matt would join us. He did.

Christmas vacation and the end of the semester came. I asked Matt about his grades. According to university policy, parents cannot access student grades unless the student permits parent access. Matt was non-committal about how many credits he'd earned. Not too many, I concluded. His apathy was apparent. He explained it away, saying that all the students were apathetic, and he didn't have the power to be different.

But it seemed to me that his apathy reached deeper and paralyzed with greater power. In my experience, many students talk the talk of not caring in front of their peers, but most talk of caring when they converse with an adult.

Steve, Matt and I argued repeatedly and vehemently about whether Matt should return to school in January.

On Christmas Eve I convinced my family, Steve, Matt,

Phillip and Carolyn, that the only thing I wanted for Christmas was for us to be in church together. I did not know if Matt and Phillip would come. They might not get off work or they might determine to spend time with friends though I did not understand why those friends would not be spending time with their families.

We all ended up in church; the same church auditorium that the baccalaureate service had been held in. I sat next to Matt who slouched, arms crossed in his chair. I worried about how he might growl at anyone who inquired about his first semester at college. Other college freshmen were present, home from college, radiating the glow that shines from the newly successful. Our son radiated fear and anger.

Toward the end of the service, everyone present lit Christmas candles and sang in unison about light shining in darkness, the hopes and fears of all the years and souls finding worth. While we sang, a message swelled inside of me and filled me: remember your prayer? The Ephesians 3 prayer about strength and love and God's company?

Of course, I remembered the prayer. I'd been praying it daily for seven months. The message continued: It's not going to look like it for a while, but your prayer has been answered.

The message wasn't audible. It was just there, branded on my knowing. And it seemed like the words were from God, but I wasn't certain.

I wanted someone to confirm that the message had been from God. I asked my pastor, "Does God speak to people like that? Was that God?"

"Maybe." He didn't commit.

I asked a friend who said with conviction, "I think it was God. If it was you conjuring up a message, you wouldn't make yourself wait."

She was right about one thing. I wouldn't make myself wait.

I noticed that the intense drive that had compelled me to pray the Ephesians prayer day after day was gone. And I knew for certain that life began to look like God had not heard my prayer at all.

Chapter four: Tsunami

In January 2006, Matt insisted on continuing at college. I think he wanted distance—a great big gap—between him and Steve and me. For him, going to college seemed the easiest way to ensure that space. His dorm was only a few miles from home. But that was far enough. He could dodge day-to-day interaction with us by ignoring the calls when our numbers flashed on his cell phone screen.

His desire for distance didn't seem all bad to me. Some kids need space to grow. And Matt was so definite about returning to college that I thought he might find a way to succeed. "I'm going to declare a major. I'll find something I like. I'll go to class. No one ever notices if I'm there or not, but I'll go."

I knew he could succeed at Penn State. And I knew what it would take to do so. An introvert like me who has succeeded at teaching mandatory writing classes to students who'd initially, at least, rather be somewhere else, knows a couple of things about surviving as an anonymous individual at a large university. It is easy to get lost in the crowd. It is easier to fail than to navigate the bureaucracy. Navigation takes effort.

Early in my stint at Penn State, I expressed nervousness about succeeding and my brother had reminded me: most of life is showing up. So show up. Day after day. I repeated that advice emphatically to Matt. Just show up. Even when no one notices.

The day before second semester classes began, I drove

Matt to his dorm. I pulled the car near the curb by the building entrance, popped the trunk and turned on the four-way blinkers. "I think the car will be okay here. I'll help you carry your stuff up."

He jumped out and gathered the bulk of his stuff from the trunk. He draped a bulging duffle bag on one arm. He grabbed a laundry basket heaped with a tangle of clean, unfolded clothes. He surveyed the rest of the stuff, "Can you get the rest?"

I could. I gathered two blankets, a pillow, a pair of sneakers, and a plastic bag filled with toothpaste, deodorant and other necessities.

He swiped his identification card to get inside the dorm and let the door swing shut behind him.

I hurried. My arms were full, so I maneuvered to rap repeatedly on the glass door with my elbow. The rap didn't draw his attention. I waited for him to realize that I was locked out. The stuff began to slip from my arms. Long minutes passed. When he didn't come back, I set my armload down, fished my cell phone from my pocket and called his.

"Where are you?" he demanded.

"Locked out. The door shut behind you."

"Have someone let you in."

I looked around. There was no one in sight. Plus, I felt irked. Like I might dump the load on the ground and leave.

"You come let me in." I said.

He came, opened the door and tried to grab the load from me and bar me from the building. I wanted to see his room. I wanted to inspect the place where he lived away from the safety of home. I wanted to see glimmers of warmth or productivity. I wanted assurance that my son could succeed in this space. Was the son I once knew showing up in this room?

Grudgingly, he let me in. Inside the room, he dumped the basket of clean, but unfolded clothes on his unmade bed and started to fold them. I grabbed a t-shirt to smooth and fold so I could stick around for a minute. I think it was the t-shirt he'd been handed at college orientation. It was stamped with a slogan that read "It's your time."

While I smoothed it, I looked around and rifled my brain for ideas to help Matt embrace this time, this opportunity. "Do you need anything? School Supplies?"

"I've got leftovers from last semester."

I tossed the folded t-shirt back his way and glanced around the room. There were no posters on the wall. No throw rugs on the cold, shiny, impersonal, impervious tile floor. The floor seemed to shout: people will come. People will go. None will leave their mark on me. Everything that is bleak and unresponsive and uncaring about a large institution coalesced in that floor. I hated that floor.

There was no homey feel in that room. On the built-in desk, I noted the barely disturbed pile of school supplies I'd bought Matt for fall semester. I fished a stapler, still wrapped in plastic, from the pile and started to tug on the wrapping. "You should carry this little stapler in your backpack. Students are always needing a stapler. You can lend yours. It's a good way to make friends."

"You can leave now, Mom."

"Will your roommate be here soon?"

"I don't even know if he's coming back this semester."

"You don't talk about things like that?"

"He's not my girlfriend."

I wrapped my arms around Matt for a hug goodbye. He let me, but his arms stayed limp at his sides. I squeezed him warmly. He didn't respond.

"Let me know if you need anything else."

"I could probably use some snacks. I don't like to eat in the cafeteria. I don't really know anyone to sit with."

"Take that little stapler to class and after someone borrows it, ask which cafeteria they eat in. Ask if you could join them for lunch." I brimmed with good ideas and seethed with pain.

We birth kids and gently strap them in bouncy chairs and encourage them with smiles and exaggerated coos. We stroke the arches of their smooth, little feet and they smile. We coax them to walk on those feet and we cheer every step. Then somewhere along the way, walking, once a parade of triumph and joy, changes from a victory lap into a wincing walk through pain. I'm not sure I prepared my kids for the pain. There is so much of it.

Sometimes, even success brandishes hurt.

I thought back to Matt's middle school years. One of his passions was basketball. He really wanted to make the middle school team. After three days of nerve-wracking try-outs, he trekked to the gym door where the list of names of individuals who'd made the team was posted. He scanned the list of twenty names. Fifty, if not more, had tried out.

Eventually, Matt saw his name on the list and felt a pop of joy. He'd made the team. He enjoyed the celebration of getting the uniform and an energy-filled weekend sleepover with a neighbor who'd made the team, too. They ate in their uniforms. They played video games in their uniforms. They slept in their uniforms.

Then Monday, at school, Matt's two best friends who had tried, but hadn't made the team, snubbed him at lunch. They wouldn't let him sit at their table. Being on the team wasn't the easiest either. The coach was demanding and unfair. Matt sat on the bench without playing a lot. Making the team was a success that marked him and the mark wasn't one of unbridled delight.

"Mom. You can leave now."

Matt's insistence intruded on my reflection. I reminded him that Penn State is a difficult place to succeed and encouraged him to search for ways to thrive. "It's not cozy here. There's no one to nurture you. You have to work diligently."

Matt positioned himself in front of something that sat on the desktop. Was he intentionally blocking my view?

"Be good and do good." I said. It was my usual parting phrase.

"Why do you have to say that?" Matt growled and pulled back from my parting hug. I was going to have to learn to keep my mouth shut. Over his shoulder, I glimpsed the weed smoking paraphernalia he'd been trying to hide from my view. I sealed my lips so not to blurt the heated scolding that rose in my being.

Matt saw the direction of my gaze. "That's not mine. It's my roommate's."

I wanted to believe him. "It's on your desk. You get caught with that and you're on your own."

I'd told him before. There are laws. If you break them, you suffer the consequences. Not me. As if I or any other mother would not suffer when her child did. Even if she watched from afar.

That was the note I left on. I didn't quite dare to hope for a successful semester.

***

I've mentioned our other son Phillip. The year Matt was a college freshman, Phillip was in tenth grade. Phillip, like all of our kids is a D.A.R.E. graduate—D.A.R.E. stands for Drug Abuse Resistance Education. Our schools used the program to teach young students, I think fifth graders, about the dangers of alcohol and drugs. Phillip once said to me, "Mom, when I was in fifth grade, I thought only murderers and robbers smoked weed. When I was in ninth grade, I realized all my friends did."

***

A couple of mornings after I'd dropped Matt off at his dorm for his second semester at college, Phillip and Steve stood side-by-side at the kitchen counter pouring coffee, toasting English muffins and chatting.

"Where's the butter?"

"We don't have any butter."

I poured myself coffee and thought about how much I despise talking for the first hour of the day. I wanted to sit in silence, but I roused myself to say, "We have butter."

"No we don't."

I opened the refrigerator door, pulled out the butter and set it in front of them.

Suppressing my remarks on evils of microwaving butter— I hate the misshapen yellow mound left in the dish once the butter is melted—I left the room with my coffee before they could voice their appreciation for my ability to find whatever they are looking for. I heard one of them open and shut the microwave door and press the start button.

It was an early Tuesday morning. The first day of classes for me that semester. Phillip headed to school to swim laps to meet a high school gym requirement. Steve headed to work. Carolyn caught her bus and I headed to campus.

Two hours later, the high school principal called Steve. I think it was the first time he'd been summoned by a principal for a kid-related matter. Our kids had earned a few less than stellar grades, a detention here and there, but nothing that prompted a telephone call from the principal. On Steve's cell. During work hours. "Your son is here at school. He's drunk. Will you pick him up?"

Steve wondered how Phillip had managed to get drunk in two short hours. And why instead of swimming his laps he'd indulged in a drinking spree.

Steve headed to the high school and on the way worked up an anger and a strong intent to hold Phillip responsible for this odd misbehavior. Steve planned to start by requiring Phillip to reimburse him for the time he was missing at work.

When Steve strode into the school, he didn't see Phillip. Steve was jarred to see disheveled, bleary-eyed Matt dressed in jeans and an unbuttoned flannel sitting on a bench outside the principal's office, looking quite lost.

"Why are you here? Why aren't you on campus?"

Matt wasn't at the high school for class.

Steve described the essence of their interaction in a frantic voicemail that I played between classes. "Matt turned up drunk at the high school this morning." The message unsettled my stomach and made meeting new students more challenging than it usually is.

Who shows up drunk at eight thirty in the morning at a place they couldn't wait to leave behind? These days, my answer is: a troubled kid who's struggling in unseen ways. That day, I thought my son was willfully choosing wrong. Steve thought so, too.

Our foolish kid broke his promise to try to succeed at

school. I was so embarrassed. He was underage. I was grateful the school administrators hadn't called the police. That seemed like a helpful lenience.

Steve reported that after Matt climbed in the truck he had said, "Dad, I'm sorry."

Steve, feeling angry and embarrassed, blurted his first reaction, "Sorry doesn't cut it. That's the easy way out. You've got to start toeing the line."

And when Steve pulled the truck to a stop at a red light, Matt jumped out and ran.

"Where did he run?" I asked when I returned Steve's call.

"I don't know. Do you think I should look for him?"

"Can you leave work? I can't cancel class today. I'm meeting these students for the first time."

Steve started his search at the dorm where he skirted security measures and rapped on the door of Matt's room. Matt wouldn't open the door but mumbled that he was there and he was safe. Steve told him to sleep his hangover off and asked the resident assistant to look in on Matt later. The resident assistant promised he would. Later, we tried to contact Matt, but he held us at arm's length.

At the time, the situation, while unpleasant, didn't seem like a gateway to a slide to disaster. An underage, drunk, wandering Matt alarmed us, but to that point the incident was a one-time thing. At that time, I often thought that maybe Matt's experience in learning to live on his own at college would mirror his attempts and eventual success at riding a bike. He wanted to ride a two wheeled bike when he was five years old. The bike we had was a little large for him. With training wheels, he could maneuver it, but when the training wheels were removed and he tried to ride, he fell. Often. He'd beg me to hold the bike upright and run behind him to get him started. I did until my back hurt from bending over and I couldn't bear to watch him fall again.

"We'll try again tomorrow," I'd promise. It seemed that mastering riding would take him all summer. Then one day, in the parking lot across the street from my parents' home, he started peddling furiously and stayed upright. That afternoon, he rode six miles.

I thought maybe his adjustment to college would be similar. He'd try again and succeed with a flourish.

When I tell my therapist my thoughts, she says, "You lived in so much denial. Even your prayers, I think they were a form of denial."

She doesn't want me to be circumstances' victim. She wants me to act more, and resist being bowled over. I don't want to be a victim and I don't want my son to be evil's victim. Could we have maneuvered these circumstances another way?

My prayers, even if they were a form of denial, were all I had. My prayers and fear.

I was so afraid. When I think back, I try to discern exactly what I feared. Was my fear founded? At the time I couldn't tell because the circumstances of our lives had catapulted from what I considered prudent and normal into an unfamiliar zone. I lived on high alert and flailed in the murk of fear and disappointment.

My life had been normal and then it was not. It was like I had been a swimmer at the shore on a sunny, hot beach day. I stood in waist-deep water batting at the waves with my hands and watching for a wave that I could joyously ride to the beach. Without warning, a tsunami rose up, rolled in, submerged me and drove me into the sand.

The wave of alien circumstances swept away my ordered, fairly happy life. As I somersaulted haphazardly in the force, part of me knew prayer was my only chance of getting righted.

Our lives began to unfold in a pattern. Something outside the boundaries of normal—like an early morning phone call and Matt showing up at the high school drunk—would happen. I'd feel afraid and pray fiercely. The fear felt bigger, more influential, than prayer. Fear piled on little fear after little fear and squeezed me inside. For certain, I learned that an early morning phone call from an unfamiliar number doesn't mean good news. When the phone rang, I'd cower.

Chapter five: New Normal

About two months passed. Eight weeks into the semester, on a Saturday morning, I was asleep. The phone, a landline, began to ring. Repeatedly. As I became more and more alert, I remembered that Steve was out of town on a fishing trip. Phillip and Carolyn had slept at friend's homes. I was the only one home to answer the phone. If it didn't stop ringing, I'd have to get up. To reach it, I pushed back the covers and trotted down a flight of stairs.

I picked up the phone, but before saying hello, I glanced at the caller identification. It read: State College Police Department. I was accustomed to calls from the Ferguson Township Police Department. They often called Steve, who works as a road superintendent, for road-related matters like malfunctioning traffic lights, traffic cone set-up or missing gas pump keys. I hoped this call was related to road matters.

"Hello," I said tentatively.

"Hello, this is Officer So and So from the State College Police Department. Is this Mrs. McDonald?"

At that moment, I knew the call wasn't about street signs or potholes.

"We have your son, Matthew Joshua McDonald, in custody for—"

I wish I could recall that officer's name. But the word custody, linked with my son's name, in a sentence, confused my thoughts and launched a contest of fear in me. All my stored feelings associated with police vied for attention and control.

I don't interact with police often. When I was ten years old, a Royal Canadian Mounted Police officer came to our family home. I peeked from behind the living room picture window drapes as the officer, handcuffs and gun strapped to his thick hip, trudged up our front walk. He looked forbidding. My mom shooed me from the living room as my dad invited the grim caller in to sit down. I overhead, not the words, but the low growl of the solemn request. I learned later that the officer had asked my dad, a pastor, to accompany him to inform a family that their son had been killed in a hunting accident. Since then, police officers loom in my mind as large, clanking bearers of catastrophic news.

I see them as emotionally unmovable, too. When I was in my early twenties, I was cited for going nine miles an hour over the speed limit in a school zone. I was going twenty-four. The limit was fifteen. The fine cost a huge chunk of cash that I could barely spare. I cried. I don't cry much. With people that know me, my tears create a wide swath of kindness in which I can regroup. My tears did not dent the officer's stern demeanor.

When Matt was six, he was riding in the back seat of our blue Phoenix. I was riding in front and Steve was driving. He accelerated through a yellow light and was pulled over. Matt and I both cowered in our seats as the officer strode purposefully to the driver's side window and rendered Steve all respectful, "Yes, Sir. No, Sir". When the officer slapped Steve with a verbal warning, Matt declared, "Well, Dad, I guess you'll never do that again."

If only.

Of course, I didn't think about those memories, but I felt the feelings they'd evoked in a big way. That officer probably never talked to a citizen so awed by his power. I felt like a misshapen mound of microwaved butter.

"Ma'am." The officer politely spoke into the silence. We were still talking by phone. "I get off in a few minutes, but I'll wait and release him to your custody, if you can come pick him up. I'd like to release him to your custody."

I drove to the station feeling numb. My thoughts were muddled. I pushed through the large glass door of the borough building. In the lobby, I looked around for the door marked with the police emblem. I felt very nervous. For me, the act of pushing the door open to the police office was like riding up that first long roller coaster hill, but the expectation of fun was replaced with the expectation of doom.

I entered and whispered to the receptionist that I was there to pick up my son. She didn't ask me to speak up.

The officer entered the room and asked me to sign a paper. I don't know what it said.

He said he'd go to the cell to get Matt. To hear cell and Matt in the same sentence was the top of the roller coaster hill. I plummeted off the side into a fall that didn't end for a long time.

The officer looked me over when he brought Matt into the room. I think he knew I was in free-fall. He tried to catch me, "This is unfortunate. But it's normal college behavior. It's nothing we didn't do when we were in college."

He was warm and kind. I wanted to believe him.

Could this be a new normal? I've never been drunk. So to consider this situation normal was a stretch for me. This situation involved: A drunk Matt leaving a party to urinate, walking back in, wondering when the party died down, stripping to his boxers, collapsing on the couch, getting cold, traipsing up the stairs to look for a blanket, getting startled by the yelp of the home owner who had not hosted a party. Matt was in the wrong house. Matt pulled on the sweatpants the homeowner threw him and left to walk the dark streets. He was eventually picked up by the police.

My sister clipped and saved the newspaper article that described the debacle. "Someday," she told me over the telephone, "you'll look back and laugh at this." Her past included more room for out-of-the-box behavior than mine.

I'm not laughing yet. But at regular intervals, I'm thankful for a homeowner who yelped and threw sweatpants at a drunken trespasser. I've read of people who killed in self-defense for less.

As for a new normal? Mine was a wary sense of impending doom.

Oh, I almost forgot to tell what else happened that day. I

took Matt home from the police station. We drove in silence. In his bedroom, he slept the drunken stupor off while I puzzled about how to present the news to Steve. Welcome home from fishing! Matt's been fined and is losing his license for three months...and the officer says his behavior is normal college behavior.

Steve's past includes more alcohol and substances than mine. Maybe considering this normal wouldn't be an awkward stretch for him. But I was nervous that he'd be angry.

Matt woke up from his day long nap with a request and a confession. "Can you drive me to my dorm? But by the way, I haven't been going to classes."

He watched for my reaction.

"What do you mean? You mean you didn't go to class last week?"

"I mean," he thought about how to tell me. "I haven't been going to classes all semester."

"You mean that you went the first week and you didn't like the classes and you didn't go back?"

"No. I mean that I never, ever went to any class."

I had heard of rumors of kids who enrolled in college and neglected to attend class, but I had never imagined that I'd meet one. Much less, be related to one.

"What have you been doing?"

"Working." He washed dishes at a local restaurant. "And..."

Years later, he told me what else he had been doing. That day I didn't press him. My perspective was suffering a seizure. I didn't need any more upheaval.

To that point, I'd thought that only irresponsible fools signed up for college and didn't go to class. People who were different from me, so different that I couldn't comprehend that course of action.

It was like after decades of life I'd been told that Mondays didn't exist.

"But I've been living Mondays."

"No chance. They don't exist."

Or like I was at the zoo, looking at a living, moving

creature that was half grass, half bones and fur. I was so perplexed.

"I guess college isn't for you," I said.

It seemed like we'd reached a dead end. I felt a multi-faceted disappointment. My emotions bounced and clattered on this disappointment's facets. I hurt in so many places.

When, as my therapist recommended, I set out to process this hurt, I put it into words to gain new perspective and dismantle the disappointment's power, I discovered that the pain recalled is so different from the pain in the moment. I realized I had set myself up for disappointment by entertaining unrealistic, rigid expectations. Part of the expectations were set by a culture that demands that young people stream to college, even though forced higher education might be a pathway to their squelching. I bought in. I said that I believed in other paths to success, but I promoted one path to success. I shouldn't have.

I compared my son's college experience to that of my friends' kids. I felt like everyone else's kid accepted the portion of the dream they were offered. Despite my coaxing from the sidelines, "It's your time! Take your portion of success and own it," my kid spurned the chance. I worried that he'd live to regret it.

Since then, I have adjusted to the disappointment of Matt not succeeding at college. I think. Every now and then I wonder about Matt going back to college. And succeeding. Is that something he needs to do? Is that an imperative stretch on the road to success? Compared to his peers, will he always feel less-than because he hasn't earned a college degree?

From this distance, dealing with the disappointment seems so easy. So he didn't meet my expectations? Change them.

So he doesn't meet our culture's benchmarks? Step back and readjust. The benchmarks are our culture's lie. Years into our journey, I reached understanding and surrender. But figuring out what aspects of my hopes and dreams for my kid to surrender took time, prayer, trial and error.

And still, some days, as I walk across campus with my

book bag hooked on my shoulder, the stint seems so simple to me. An individual applies to college and is accepted—the hard part. Then every single day, for the next eight semesters, he gets up and goes to class. However, I recently read in the Chronicle of Higher Education that at any given time thirty percent of current college students are so depressed that they can't climb out of bed.

Something keeps them from showing up.

And if I have something to say about that, it's this: We have to stop force-feeding our kids our dreams of a cozy, prosperous future and give them the room, opportunity and support to dare to find their life's purpose.

Chapter six: Rip Van Winkle

At semester's end, when the dorm closed, Matt moved home. Steve declared, "If you're living at home and not going to college, you work forty hours a week."

The forty-hour work week benchmark was to Steve what education was to me. Steve believed that working forty hours was imperative for life success. And the number forty was a low bar—a starting place. Steve and the people he admires regularly work far more than forty hours a week.

"Sure, Dad. I'll do that." In words, Matt agreed to Steve's requirement. In action, he worked a few hours at a part-time job at a golf course. When he wasn't working, he stayed in bed, slept and counted the days until he'd leave for Hawaii to visit one of his high school friends who had moved there to teach scuba diving. Matt had saved up money from a dishwashing job and purchased a ticket for this trip months in advance.

"Maybe we should say he can't go. As punishment." That idea was Steve's. "He needs to get his life together—not go off to vacation in Hawaii."

Steve wanted to dictate Matt's progress through life and so did I. At least parts of it. I mean families have expectations. Parents hold kids accountable.

We groped for ways to push Matt to meet our expectations. Friends and acquaintances whose kids were a few years older than ours still used rules. When people learned of Matt's dismal progress in life, many eagerly shared parenting practices that had worked for them. If my kids go to college and maintain a "B" average, then I pay their bill and provide them with a car.

Or, I tell my kids if they don't go to college after high school, and they choose to live at home, then they work forty hours a week and pay rent.

Or, I'd never charge my own kids rent, but I do tell them they must be productive. That means work or go to school.

I listened and tried to discern guidance that would apply to our situation, but I never heard a rule about a kid who refused to get out of bed.

Well, once I heard of a mother who blasted her son's trumpet—badly because she lacked a practiced aperture—in his ears until he got out of bed for school. I felt linked to her desperation, and I loved that mother. Once our family owned a sax, but no trumpets. Maybe I could try a whistle.

Sometimes, I'd go into Matt's room around eleven in the morning and say pleasantly something like, "Okay, Rip Van Winkle, time to rise and shine." When he was a young boy, I'd read aloud, more than a few times, the story of the kind old man who, to avoid his wife's nagging, slept through the American Revolution. After listening, the young boy Matt marveled that a man could sleep so long. At that time, sleep was low on his list of priorities. He didn't like to sleep because he might miss things. Now he was a sleeping young man, and I wondered what revolution he was avoiding. "Get up and face the day!" I'd chirp.

My chirping was as useless as the rusty musket Rip Van Winkle found at his side when he awoke from his nap which spanned two decades. At the sound of my voice, the young man whose physical features I knew, but whose behavior had spiked unfamiliar, would roll over and groan, "Just a little longer."

"Twenty minutes," I'd acquiesce. I'd leave him alone for forty or fifty minutes and then I'd try to rouse him again. He'd pull the pillow over his head and beg for more sleep.

"How can you possibly want more sleep? There is such a thing as too much sleep you know," I'd exclaim feeling agitated. I personally have never experienced too much sleep, but I have heard that such a phenomenon exists.

"Leave me alone." He'd roll over.

I'd sit on the edge of Matt's bed and pray for an idea to entice him to get up. Maybe a giant shoehorn?

Often the phone would ring and when I answered it, Steve would ask, "Is Matt up yet? I left a list of chores for him." My stomach would wrench.

I've always considered the option of working from home on days when I wasn't lecturing a classroom full of students a privilege and I accepted the task of tending to my kids' well-being when I was home, but those calls in which Steve tried to direct that care set me seething. Now, I realize, I should have talked to Steve more. I could have described how dreadful I felt when Matt and I couldn't meet his expectations. However, at the time, we were all tangled in serpentine strong, dark emotions that strangled healthy communication.

In that emotional tangle, I felt angry that Steve tried to manage from afar. His directive increased the helplessness I felt. In the course of my day, before the call, I felt incompetent to get Matt moving. The call magnified that feeling. Because I knew I'd have to report failure at the end of the day, I also felt an overshadowing sense of doom.

Sometimes, I felt that if I could coax Matt to get up and do a couple of productive things, like apply for a job or complete a chore or two from Steve's list, I could get Steve off both our backs.

Matt's upcoming trip to Hawaii seemed like a potential respite from these oppressive feelings. I thought that if Matt was in Hawaii for three weeks, Steve wouldn't call me with his list. I'd enjoy three weeks of peace.

When Steve mentioned requiring Matt to stay at home, I said, "What? Have him stay here and fight with you?"

The Sunday before Matt's trip, he agreed to attend church with us. He hadn't been since Christmas Eve and since we are an every-Sunday-in-church kind of family that seemed like a long stretch without church. We didn't pressure him to accompany us. He could have extended his absence streak and excused himself from participating by claiming a need to pack; however, he joined us willingly. While I sat next to him in church my hopes surged. I thought: Matt could meet God in church that day and that meeting could solve everything. God could fortify Matt, infuse him with joy; and draw him back to family, God, and life as I planned it. To avoid disappointment, I tried to quell my expectations.

The bewildering direction Matt's life had taken had caused me to question some of the values I'd staunchly held, but I still knew for sure: God is present in church. And people attend because God's presence makes a difference for them. Sure, people can go to church and not meet God, but choosing to attend was a step in a positive direction and I hadn't seen Matt move that way in a long time.

The services' flaws tempered my cheer. The worship seemed plodding and sour. The singers sang out of tune and between songs the worship leader droned on in boring narration. If God was present, attendees didn't seem impressed. I wanted to lean over and whisper an apology in my son's ear. I wanted to murmur an effective prompting; a message to urge his attention to God. Look beyond this ineptness, please!

It was communion Sunday. Once every month at the conclusion of the regular service which included singing, praying and preaching, the communion rite was observed at our church. Plates of bread cubes and silver trays filled with tiny glasses of grape juice were passed to people who remained seated in their rows engaged in self-examination and prayer. Individuals could take or pass the bread and juice as they wished without drawing attention to their participation, or lack of it. But that Sunday, the format differed. The bread and grape juice were spread on tables which were set in the corners of the auditorium. Individuals who desired communion were to walk from their seats to the tables and help themselves to the bread and juice. Music played softly.

I viewed communion as a solemn occasion requiring reverence and intent to follow God and his ways. The scripture the pastor read to preface the act invited people to participate and warned that people should consider the state of their souls before doing so.

"Whoever participates in an unworthy manner will be guilty of sinning against the body and blood of the Lord," the pastor said. The warning settled on me heavy, like a lead apron. The grave sense of woe and doom dwarfed the invitation.

I was certain that Matt could not examine himself—he was hostile, lazy and pursued substance highs—and conclude that his lifestyle met a suitable standard for participating, so I determined to exclude myself. If he couldn't celebrate, I wouldn't celebrate. While I prayed, Matt stirred and walked past me.

I grabbed the fabric of his shirtsleeve and tugged. "Where are you going?" I hissed.

"Communion," he growled back. I grew alarmed. Didn't he understand the warning? Or was he ignoring it? Why would that surprise me? Ignoring warnings seemed to be his current, usual practice. And part of me rejoiced that he still cared about celebrating Jesus. I caught up to and tailed him to the communion table. We sipped the grape juice, chewed the bread morsel and, standing awkwardly by the table, prayed together for safety on his trip.

When I left church that day, I felt pummeled by strong emotions. I worried because Matt ignored God's standards. I fretted about possible consequences of that behavior. On the other hand, I wanted to celebrate Matt's participation in church and communion as a golden ticket of indication: All is not lost. He believes! I felt compelled to curb my celebration because his actions did not, in my estimation, coincide with belief.

We watch our kids for signs of faith. For indications that things that matter most to us also matter to them. Do we want to replicate ourselves? Or is it that we've struggled and found soothing answers to the questions of life and death and we want to share the balm?

For so many years, worry about Matt's soul consumed and weakened me. I wondered about the position and posture of his soul in this battle for his life. I worried. What if he died while dabbling in the dark side of life?

I thought and prayed about that a lot. When I look back, I

wonder if I was fabricating a catastrophe. He wasn't a crime lord, or a vicious villain looting and ravaging unarmed helpless people. He wasn't Hannibal Lector. He was a kid who had lost his way.

He did not act as a steward of the good things God gave him. In fact, he acted like an anti-steward. He destroyed his own body. He smoked cigarettes and other substances. He drank a lot of alcohol. Secretly and often. Sometimes, he stole alcohol. He didn't participate in productive activity. When Matt interacted with people, he was curt, sullen, and selfish. He could not see beyond his own very basic needs. If he interacted at all, the interaction was laced with hostility.

Here's the thing: until he was about seventeen, Matt had been on track to care and share. But that impulse had been hijacked. Nothing I said or did could convince him to attempt to participate in life.

I thought he might return from his three week visit to Hawaii with new vigor. On his return, I drove four hours from central Pennsylvania to pick him up at the Cleveland airport. I anticipated a friendly reunion in which I'd treat him to dinner, he'd thank me and he'd share details and pictures of his trip. As a bonus, he'd reveal that he had found purpose.

I pulled up to the curb at the airport terminal and got out of the car to hug him. He sauntered towards me. His greasy hair still hung shoulder length, his scowl seemed deeper, and he and his backpack reeked, "Put that in the trunk!" I ordered. "Didn't they have showers there?"

"I'm hungry. I ran out of money for food the last couple days."

I considered a restaurant, but he wanted a drive-through. "I'm tired. I want to eat and then sleep while you drive."

I didn't really want to sit across from this disheveled looking, foul-smelling tramp in public anyway. I'd feel compelled to excuse his appearance and bearing to a server. The drive-through would work.

He gobbled a double cheeseburger in four bites. He pushed four fries at a time into a plastic single serving tub of ketchup and then crammed them into his mouth, chewing slightly. He guzzled a liter of soda. His eating etiquette appalled me. In between bites, he showed me a few pictures of a volcano and beaches and thrust a small paper bag at me. "It's not much. I picked it up in the airport gift shop on my way off the island. I didn't take much time to pick it out, either. Probably you won't like it."

He was right. The light blue plumeria strung on a silver chain is not me. In any other circumstance, I would scorn that necklace. But I loved that he thought of me while in Hawaii and ten years later? I wear that necklace regularly.

He slept most of the drive from Cleveland to State College. He woke up once, urgently needing a restroom. After our quick stop, we chatted for a few minutes before he went back to sleep.

During that chat, Matt told me that God spoke to him in Hawaii. He was staying with a high school friend and his roommates. They spent most their time partying—drinking beer, smoking weed and ingesting other substances. They did a little sight-seeing and hiking.

One day, Matt took some time away from the group. Alone, he hiked up a small mountain into a pineapple field. "It's really beautiful there, Mom. You should go sometime."

In the field, Matt sat down, pulled his bible from his backpack and read verses from Psalms. While he did, he felt God's presence. He said it was like God tapped him on the shoulder and said, "I exist. I'm here. I'm real. I created everything you see."

In response, the thought of abandoning partying crossed Matt's mind, "I considered walking down from that mountain and saying to my friends, 'there's more to life than partying. We should look for more.'"

Even so, when we arrived home in State College, Matt walked in the house, deposited his backpack in front of the washer, grunted hello to other family members and crawled into bed.

I thought about his detailed description of his time on the mountainside. I could picture rich brown soil, the green plants and the blue ocean in the distance. I wondered if the scent of pineapple filled the air. I wondered what compelled him to leave his partying friends and climb the mountain with his bible. I was thankful that God had spoken to him.

But he reported ignoring the message.

All my life, I'd heard of consequences of ignoring God. In a childhood full of Sunday mornings spent in Sunday school in a Canadian Baptist church where the diminutive, stern Sunday School Superintendent Miss Oshiro used many methods to familiarize her pupils with the bible, I'd learned that ignoring God is not recommended.

One game Miss Oshiro used to increase students' familiarity with the bible was called Sword Drill. The game is based on a verse in Hebrews that likens the word of God to a sharp sword. The bibles that we carried to Sunday school were our swords. Miss Oshiro would command, "Draw swords."

Pupils held bibles high over their heads.

Miss Oshiro called out a bible reference: book, chapter and verse. "Romans 2:5-8. Go!"

When Miss Oshiro said go, students hurriedly paged through bibles hunting for the verse. The first to find it jumped to his or her feet. The reward was reading the verse aloud for all to hear.

I think the church I grew up in taught a rich theology and the verses we read represented that, but as a rule-following child, the message I heard most prominently was stern, like the message declared in Roman 2:5-8

> But because of your stubbornness and your unrepentant heart, you are storing up wrath against yourself for the day of God's wrath, when his righteous judgment will be revealed. 6 God "will repay each person according to what they have done" 8 But for those who reject the truth, there will be wrath and anger.

The understanding was seared into my being: an individual who hears God's voice and walks away, unmoved, courts disaster. When I considered Matt's experience on the hill in Hawaii, I wondered, does God, once ignored, speak into a life again?

Chapter seven: Stealthy Theft

My treasures have been stolen before. When I was twelve years old, my red two-wheeled bike vanished one night from the recesses of our family's carport. The bike was not costly, but I prized it. The handlebars were decked out with sprays of colorful, plastic, streamers. When I stood straddling the bike in the driveway or on the sidewalk and talked with my friends about where to ride next, I wound the streamers around my fingers creating many colorful rings. Occasionally, my friends used clothes pins to clip playing cards to their bicycle spokes and rode around our neighborhood in a clattering bike parade. My Dad warned that the playing card attachments were not a good idea. "You'll loosen the spokes," he said. Without the clattering cards, I rode on the parade's perimeter. As a self-selected outcast, I felt less cool than my friends, but I didn't want to risk my father's disapproval or loose spokes.

Once stolen, my prized bike was missing for a few days and returned broken. I sobbed when the police, who had found the bike abandoned, delivered it to our yard with the front wheel bent. If a person wanted something bad enough to steal it, why wouldn't they take care of it? I wondered. The small mark on my psyche was indelible and distinct: our safe spaces can be breached.

When my own kids were young, their over-sized, hard plastic wading pool was removed, at night, from our front yard—we'd left it full of water. A college kid's prank, I concluded. I was sure the misguided culprits stole for fun, not to dole out malice.

The theft of these minor objects would merit meager, if any, mention in a police report. Even so, the incidents angered me. The intrusions unsettled me. In both cases, the crime scene was small and well-lit. The risks of detection were high. Conjuring up the audacity to attempt the acts would require some brazen fiends.

About the pool, Carolyn who was about four years old at the time exclaimed, "We need to catch the people who did this." I agreed with her sentiment; we—my daughter and I— talk boldly about catching culprits who wrong us. We want them to pay.

A couple of winters after the pool theft, on a night when road conditions were icy, a speeding car lost control on the curve near our house, careened off the road and collided with our car which was parked, without occupants, in our driveway. Before the driver could be caught or identified, he or she sped away, leaving us with a repair bill that wasn't quite as steep as our insurance deductible.

By examining broken car parts gathered from our driveway, police determined the make, model and color of the car that hit our car. The police provided us with the information but did not seem energized to pursue the matter. The $999.99 wasn't coming out of their pockets. So Carolyn and I took solving the crime into our own hands. We pulled on coats, hats and mittens and sat in our cold car in the driveway for an hour each day. We strategically varied the time of our stakeout. We watched the cars that drove by, eager to spot a gold Honda Civic with a missing right headlight. We planned to pursue, note the license plate number and pass it to police. Or, if the situation demanded, we'd confront the driver ourselves.

Geared, as I am, to react to petty theft with outrage, to sound alarms and to campaign for the pursuit of justice, you might wonder—as, in retrospect, I wonder—why I witnessed depression's stealthy theft—the grand larceny of my son's irreplaceable essence–in cowed silence.

"Why were you silent? Why didn't you speak up?" My therapist doesn't accept the silences that are familiar cramps to me. She so believes, and wants me to believe, I can speak into life's difficult situations. I grope for an answer to her question.

Maybe I grew silent because Matt met my initial comments, geared to garner agreement and closeness, with brusque protests and cold distance.

"You don't seem like yourself," I'd say.

"Leave me alone!" he'd demand and slam his bedroom door behind him.

Maybe because my spoken dismay at Matt's off-track actions ignited Steve's anger.

"We need to do something." Steve would claim. "Maybe we should kick him out."

"What?" For some reason, Steve thought that the possibility of being kicked out of our home would motivate Matt. I refused to consider that possibility. Our discussions about Matt's demeanor and actions led to conflict. I avoided conflict because I thought it was like the playing cards that my friends clipped to their bicycle spokes—annoyingly noisy and harmful to the bonds that hold relationships together. (I've learned to think differently.)

Maybe I didn't recognize the pilferer's sinister power. In the early years, pressed for an explanation, I would have said sadly, but confidently: depression is a choice. A moral choice. Matt chooses to partner in the unfolding heist. Matt is a culprit. Not a victim.

Maybe because Matt's essence eroded so slowly. His actions, interests, loves, capabilities and conversation were interesting and detailed like the colorful designs of a kaleidoscope display. Then, bit by bit, a colorful point, or collection of points, faded. A section of colorful designs vanished. And then, another, and poof! We were left with the looming, empty shell of a person. He wasn't gone. His drooping body lingered. It settled heavy on furniture. He dragged from his bedroom to the kitchen to the couch in the living room. But his personality, his spark, seemed extinguished.

"He's flat," my sister said once. "His affect. It's just flat."

When I think back, it seems that the first feature of Matt's life to disappear was a healthy routine. From the day we brought Matt home from the hospital, we built healthy routine into our days. I like routine. I believe that we build a life to value and enjoy day by day, healthy act, by healthy act. In contrast, an unhealthy routine makes room for despair or catastrophe to enter and lure an individual to an action that results in a life of swirling regret. I might even have been a little rigid in my pursuit of routine and my proclamations. It's time to: get up, get dressed, eat breakfast, do chores, go outside to exercise or play. Lunch time. Reading time. Naptime. Dad comes home from work. That means supper and goodnight rituals. Occasionally, visits to the doctor or to a friend's home or a trip to the grocery store added variety to our schedule. And, of course, the number of activities increased as our kids grew, started school, and I returned to fulltime teaching.

Eager to start each day, Matt always got up earlier than I wanted. Always. In the beginning, I'd collect him from his crib, change his diaper, and slip back into bed with him tucked by my side. I'd kiss his forehead, stroke his soft cheeks or the chubby part at the tops of his arms, and coo, "C'mon, Sweetie, sleep. Just a little longer."

He'd fuss and squirm or do that baby thing where he'd rotate his little wrist in front of his face and stare in concentrated wonder—what is this unique moving part and how does it work?

Matt's routine and his eagerness to start each day disappeared. He chose, with a vengeance, a routine of sleep. After returning from Hawaii, he spent most of the fall in bed. Each day, he'd get up around three o'clock in the afternoon, drink a cup of coffee, pull on a hooded sweatshirt and sit in a chair on the back porch, hood on, shoulders hunched. He'd face the field that borders our yard, resolute—like, if he just peered hard enough an extravagant spectacle would appear—and, at the same time, detached— if a parade of characters twirling and reeling in acts of derring-do passed by he wouldn't notice. He'd smoke a cigarette and toss the butt into the flower garden just off the porch. Then he'd light up another. A mound of butts accumulated in the mulch—indisputable evidence that he smoked far more each day than the one or two he claimed.

If the weather was warm, I'd join him on the porch. I'd pause and gaze at the field, too. I'd comment on visible familiar features: shadows, grass, squirrels, the fort—barely visible—where, as a child, he'd spent hours. I'd comment on the invisible—distant happy memories of times spent in that field.

"Remember when you used to ride your go-cart round and round out there?"

He rebuffed my every effort to remind him of a happier time. I wasn't trying to be mean. I wanted to remind him of the possibilities of happiness. He had known happiness before, and he could know it and link arms with it again. After a spell of non-response, I'd decide to move on.

"Clean up your butts," I'd gently prod before leaving him.

"Clean up those butts!" Steve bellowed if he was around. "How much money do those cigarettes cost you?"

Now and then, Matt raked up the butts. More often, after he left for work, when no one else was home I'd sigh, pull on rubber gloves, squat, or kneel in the garden, and pick the unsightly pieces of shrapnel from the mulch. Snow was helpful. It hid the debris. Now and then, Steve or I placed an ashtray on the back-porch table, shoved it in front of Matt and commanded, "Use this."

But neither of us liked to see the pile of discarded, crooked butts that steadily accumulated in the dish.

"You denied so much." My therapist says. Again.

I hear her. "That's denial? I was just trying to eke out a life. I was trying to find a way to keep on living despite the overwhelming indications that things were not right. I thought denial meant believing a problem didn't exist. I knew we had a problem. But talking about it only made it worse."

After his daily cigarette, or two, Matt left for his dishwashing job at a local restaurant. I think the shift was four to eleven, but he didn't get home until long after midnight.

While I waited for him, I tossed and turned in bed, shifting from side to side, pulling the sheets up to my chin, poking my too-hot feet out from under the covers. I didn't sleep. I learned what it's like to live robbed of sleep. During those years, I realized how cumbersome arms are to a sleepless individual. When I rolled to my side, my arm was an awkward bump preventing me from sinking into the mattress. Stretched out on my back, I tried folding my hands over my stomach with my elbows tucked in at my waist. I tried laying with my arms straight at my sides or stretched over my head, my hands grasping the headboard spindles. I couldn't find a graceful space to cradle my arms.

And then I'd hear the crunch of the tires on the driveway signaling Matt's return. He'd come inside. I'd hear muffled clunks of movement in the kitchen: the knock of the cupboard doors opening and closing, the clatter of silverware, and the scrape of a stool across the tile. The ice dispenser grinding and dropping cubes into a glass sounded so loudly—a flurry of clapping cards rattling inside my head. Television voices blurted loud and vacuous. I'd smell toast. After a few minutes, I'd hear the shower.

Beside me in bed, Steve snored. I was glad he slept, because if he woke up, he'd be angry at Matt's noise. Of course, I'd have rather been sleeping, too. But since I was awake, based on the noises, I mapped Matt's routine in my mind. He was home. A few minutes after the shower, I'd hear him open the door to the back porch. If our bedroom window was open, I'd smell the cigarette smoke that wafted my way and signaled that he'd soon head to bed. My arms could settle into a space. I could sleep. Most nights. Sometimes, the cigarette smoke preceded a late-night car trip. I'd hear Matt's tires crunch on the gravel as he left the driveway. And though I told myself again and again: Bars close at two. He can't get alcohol anywhere at this time. I could not lull myself to rest. I was robbed of peace. My worries grew more unwieldy than my arms: my son had exchanged healthy routine for days that started and ended with cigarettes. And those were the good days.

Chapter eight: Compensating

A mother has got to know when to worry. So in May 2015, when, after graduating from college, our youngest child, our daughter, Carolyn, the one who'd sat with me in the car on the stakeouts, moved to the volatile city Port-au-Prince, Haiti, I signed up for email news alerts from the United States embassy in Haiti.

Frequently, security messages geared to US citizens, warning of active demonstrations with potential to escalate into violent situations, flood my inbox. When I read the warnings, I text Carolyn an alert, "Demonstration in Petionville. Are you safe?"

She responds, "Demonstrations are not dangerous. Only worry if they say roadblocks."

"Not my question. Are you safe?"

One day, she texted from her apartment that she was bored and confined there because demonstrators who were distraught over politics mobbed the nearby streets, setting tires on fire in some of them. "I can hear the demonstrations."

"You're staying inside? Right?" Inside, she'd be safe, I told myself. But then I wondered about those burning tires. What were the chances of the flames igniting nearby buildings and setting a block of buildings, or a city, on fire? Haiti does not have a 911 system in place, so who would she dial for help? In the long, silent interval before her next text message, I reminded myself that Carolyn is responsible and fluent in the language and that pursuing interests, even interests that include great risk, is preferable to living without interests.

I know this truth because I watched helplessly while depression stole more than Matt's routine. It stripped him of all interests. Matt began life as a curious, engaged individual. He performed self-designed experiments on items and people. I'll never forget the day I carefully placed Phillip, Matt's baby brother—who could wave his arms and legs, but couldn't roll—on a soft blanket in the middle of the carpeted living room and hurried to the tiled kitchen (the difference in floor surfaces was the reason I didn't bring him with me. I thought the soft surface would be more comfortable.) to make coffee. When I heard Phillip coughing, I rushed back to the living room to see three-year-old Matt, brow crinkled in concentration, kneeling, draped over Phillip's head with his fingers in Phillip's mouth.

"Why is the baby coughing," I asked as I scooped Phillip up.

"Because I'm trying to get this dime out of his mouth," Matt explained. With a flourish, he waved his success—a wet coin—between his thumb and forefinger.

I didn't ask how the dime had gotten into the baby's mouth. Reminded that Matt's curiosity was unbounded, I resolved to practice more vigilance.

When he is healthy, Matt's interests are too many to list: sports—participant and spectator, outdoor activities—hiking and biking, church, reading, woodworking, pets—especially dogs.

But as depression gripped him, his interests shriveled and then disappeared. His inner being was confined in a narrow, bland space.

In the mornings, when I'd urge him out of bed, I'd chirp a list of things he once liked. "There's a day waiting to be lived. You can walk the dog or go to the bookstore and find an interesting book to read. There's bacon! You can cook bacon for breakfast. Or give Grandma and Grandpa a call." When my urging didn't work and I can't recall a time it did, my worry grew. I'd plead. I'd pray. I'd beg.

"Rub my back. And then I'll get up," Matt would say.

I thought he chose to stay in that bed. I didn't know why. Getting up seems like such a simple task. You fold back the covers. Turn your legs over the side of the bed and with a slight push—and wow!—you're standing.

Some days, after trying to rouse him every twenty or thirty minutes for hours, I'd retreat to my bedroom, get on my knees and pray so desperately. Or wail. Or sob. "God Almighty, please, please help."

When Matt finally got up, he'd trot downstairs. Trotting downstairs is a habit that he inherited from me. I inherited it from my mother. When she was in her prime, she took flights of stairs at a quick run. I considered Matt's trotting a good sign. Part of him still existed.

In the kitchen, he'd make breakfast. Often, bacon and eggs. The sounds of him cooking, the smell of the food built a flimsy card house of hope in my heart. He was being erased more and more each day, but part of his essence still existed.

After giving him time to eat, to prevent him from plopping down on the couch, closing his eyes and shutting life out, I'd strategically intervene. I'd suggest a chore or an activity to try to entice him back to life.

"The dog needs a walk."

"Or, we really need milk. Could you go get it?"

"Or, look. Here's a newspaper article about Penn State football." The talking was all me, but Penn State football always piqued his interest for a few minutes. Ever since I can remember, Matt has actively enjoyed Penn State Football. Many times, dressed in blue or white, with a 100,000 cheering fans, he'd attended the best show in college football at Beaver Stadium. Thanks to one of his uncles, he enjoyed the game seated at the 50-yard line. He filled in the blank in the "We are..." chant and bent enthusiastically in the Penn State stadium wave before he was ten.

If he couldn't attend in person, he watched the game on television. He knew the players' names and positions. He educated me on their abilities and talked Penn State football statistics as effortlessly as I say the alphabet.

He always read the Penn State articles I pointed out. Once in a while, he'd comment on them. And then one day, that changed.

I had planned to go to lunch with a friend. She called to confirm and she heard the waver in my voice, "What's wrong?"

"My son's not doing well today. I know it sounds dumb, but I hate to leave him alone for too long."

"Invite him to come with us?"

"I don't think he'd do that."

Instead of lunch, we agreed to meet at a park near our home for a short walk. As we trudged the path that circles the park, I recalled times I'd visited the park with the kids. I'd sit on a bench, with a book and they'd play. I'd caution Matt from swinging too high or climbing too precariously on playground equipment or I'd call to him as he dribbled on the basketball court, "It's dark. It's time to go home. There's not light for one more basket."

My friend and I walked in silence for a while. My eyes filled with tears. I could barely explain, "He used to greet everything with enthusiasm and today after I coaxed him out of bed, placed the newspaper, opened to an article on the upcoming Penn State Football game in front of him, he pushed the paper away and said flatly, 'I don't like Penn State Football.' He shuffled into the living room, laid down on the couch and closed his eyes."

During the time and in the space where Matt had no interests, Steve and I felt stifled. Depression's tentacles gripped us, too. Sometimes, I could barely breathe.

"You seem so passive." My therapist said. "There are lots of articles on learned helplessness."

I had never heard that term, "learned helplessness", but when she says it, the concept strikes recognition. And when I look up the definition? I note with interest that my experience is shared and labeled. Learned helplessness occurs when an individual's experience creates the expectation that nothing he or she does will have an impact. The individual feels helpless and begins to act in a helpless manner even when he or she could act to make things different.

Ouch. And well. Well. Well. Hmm.

At first, I wasn't passive. But so many times Steve or I tried to get Matt moving, to re-ignite his interests and our actions ended in failure and conflict.

Once, desperate to pry Matt off the couch, I invited him to accompany Carolyn, two of my nieces and me on a hike. The twelve-year-old girls expressed ambivalence about the hike. They wanted to stay home and watch a movie called Jumanji. I wasn't sure the movie was appropriate and, repeatedly, I insisted that the hike would be more enjoyable and beneficial. I planned to visit the Alan Seeger Natural Area in the Rothrock Forest and I told Matt the outing wouldn't be complete unless he joined us.

"I don't feel like hiking."

"You love this hike. You've always loved it."

"I don't even remember this hike."

"The Alan Seeger Area? The rhododendrons? The big trees?"

The story might be a rural legend, but I have heard that the Alan Seeger Area was the only patch of woods in Pennsylvania that hadn't burned to the ground in a forest fire that swept Pennsylvania three or four centuries ago. Spared again in the near-universal logging of the nineteenth century, the white pine and hemlock trees—some date back to the 1500's—are robust and solid and soar straight and tall to the sky. The light that infiltrates the green lacey canopy created by the hemlocks seems filled with peace and promise. The space acts like a natural cathedral to me. Visiting there lifts my spirits and inspires reverence. The hike is easy—a mile walk that circles near a stream that makes music in the vast outdoors.

"It will be good to be outside," I inflated my tone with heartiness to build up participant enthusiasm. Matt agreed to come. The girls scraped up some zeal. I packed a snack for us to eat at the picnic area. As we headed out the door, Matt plunked down on the couch. He'd decided to stay home.

It was hard for me to leave him. Honestly, sometimes I thought I should just move another couch into the living room and lay down, too.

But I'd talked the girls into hiking. I wanted to hike. I wanted a life. Building one seemed an unfamiliar and cumbersome task. As a mother, I'd spent a large portion of my time and energy focused on providing a good life for my kids. I'd lived my life—done the "me" things—in the margins, with the resources that were left after the kids had what they needed.

But when no margin opens because one kid is stalled and all time, all attention and all energy isn't sufficient to get him moving? When you can't get his well-being checked off and move to the me-margins? Every resource I had couldn't get what seemed to be the main task started, and I had no room, energy, or motivation to attempt the margin task of building a life. For me.

But that day, I decided that since the girls were anticipating the hike, since I had talked it up, I would leave Matt on the couch.

As I tore myself away, I experienced very nervous feelings about what might happen when he was left alone. Sometimes, he made self-destructive decisions. Once, I found an empty cough syrup bottle in the ashes of a campfire that he'd had one evening. Ingested in high quantities some cough syrups cause individuals to experience euphoria and hallucinations. I knew he wasn't euphoric. I wondered about hallucinations, but that's a story for another chapter.

When I showed him the empty cough syrup bottle, he declared, "It's not mine." My stomach clenched.

Consistently, the feeling that I had to be constantly present on high alert in case I needed to intervene and the feeling that I needed to find a way to have a life took turns mauling me. And, I suppose they mauled me both at once, but I could only note one or the other.

The hike day, I opted for a life. I determined that the hike would not last long and we'd go and enjoy it.

Walking in the Alan Seeger Area reminded me of the possibilities of restoration. For a few brief moments, I strolled the edges of beauty and peace. The girls exclaimed over the size of the trees and ran and hid in alcoves created by mountain laurel and balanced carefully on fallen trees. We all smiled and felt cares lifted.

After the hike, we drove to the picnic area and when the girls were getting out of the car, one of them accidently slammed the car door on Carolyn's finger. I'm certain Carolyn's piercing shriek set on high alert creatures that had been hibernating since Alan Seeger Area trees were saplings. I had thought that every part of me was operating on high alert, but the shriek set more protectiveness into high gear. I rounded the car, opened the door quickly, but could barely bring myself to look, thinking I'd see oozing blood and mangled tissue. Fortunately, the slam didn't break the skin and it wasn't until the next day that a doctor splinted the minor break in her finger. However, the agony she'd wailed blotted out the hike's beauty. I could've stayed home and felt pain. A big dose of what's-the-use? sloshed over me.

Another time, when Steve was mowing the lawn, he found three orphaned, or deserted, newly hatched baby ducks, in a nest. He carefully placed the nest in a cardboard box and showed the ducklings to Matt. They blindly groped for care by extending their scrawny necks and opening and closing their beaks.

"They'll die unless someone feeds them."

Matt has always had a heart for creatures and the sight of the babies stirred action in him. He found an eyedropper and carefully mushed worms, mixed them with water and dropped beads of nourishment into the beaks. They seemed to guzzle the concoction and perked up and chirped. Matt placed the box in a warm place, away from predators. His interest in providing life for the baby fowl warmed us. We talked about incubators and wondered where to get one.

In the morning only two babies squirmed with life. Their little beaks opened and closed. Steve disposed of the still, cold one before Matt could see it. Later that day, when Matt checked between feedings, only one was left alive. And despite his best attempt at eye dropper feeding and cooed encouragement that one died, too. Matt turned away from the cardboard box. Flat.

We scolded ourselves for inviting his interest.

And the feeling that came with witnessing his dashed interest was a dark place for me. He hadn't asked to be born. In a way, we'd invited him to life. I'd birthed a kid, with joy, fully believing life smacks of interesting things; life offers a smorgasbord of various delights, but my son found nothing to pique his interest. No matter how hard we tried. We couldn't spark his interest. And then I began to give up. I thought things like—maybe interest is overrated. What good does interest do, anyway? We all end up in the same place. Our life on earth comes to an end. So if he pursues interests along the way, or if he lays on the couch, uninterested in anything, what does it matter?

I want what I do to matter. The most important way I can do something that matters is to see that my kids find life—if I can't make that happen? That's where I learned helplessness.

So depression stole Matt's healthy routine, his interests and then it plundered his abilities.

For my kids, including Matt, growing up included a progression in which each child became more adept at completing tasks that increased in complexity and responsibility.

"I can't wait until I'm old enough to walk to school by myself."

"I want to ride my bike to the store by myself!"

"I want to drive with a friend to Florida for spring break. By ourselves."

It seems that individuals, healthy individuals, are prompted forward, prompted to grow, by the desire to do things—to assume more demanding responsibilities, more daring acts—on their own. Matt was always compelled to do more, to do it better and to expand his world with increasing responsibility. As a child, he demonstrated strong initiative, responsibility and skill.

The year he learned to ride his bike, I told him, "If you get home from school and I am not here, you may ride your bike down the road to visit Merton." Merton was an older gentleman who lived about a quarter mile from our house and enjoyed visits from our kids. "When I get home, I will come for you there."

One day, a week later, I arrived home about two short minutes behind Matt's bus. Intoxicated by the glee of independent capacity—riding his bike on his own to the neighbor's—Matt was halfway there when I pulled into our driveway.

Years later when he landed his first paying job, after cashing his first paycheck, while counting his bills, he told me, "You don't have to pay for my school lunches anymore. I can do that now."

He could take care of his brother and sister while Steve and I were out of town. He could change the oil and spark plugs on his car. In woodshop, he built a desk from scratch.

And then, during the difficult years, his capability vanished. There were mornings, when after he ate breakfast, to make the most of momentum, I'd suggest, "It's nice out. Take the dog for a walk."

Sometimes, he'd agree and leave; dog in tow. And sometimes, he'd come back with the leash dangling from his hand.

"Where is the dog?" I'd ask.

"I let him off the leash and he ran away," he shrugged, apparently unconcerned.

"You can't just do that. We'll have to look for the dog." I'd pull on my coat. He'd hand me the leash, relinquishing responsibility.

I'd protest, "You need to help."

He'd shrug and head for the couch.

I'd search for the dog by myself.

Through the worst of times, he had a job. A dishwashing job. I'm not sure how or why he held it. It was a thin thread, giving him something to do in life. The job started at 4:00. The restaurant was about a ten-minute drive from our house. At 3:55, he'd start looking for his work stuff. He needed: His apron. His grease-caked, non-skid shoes. His cap that was stamped with the restaurant emblem.

"I can't find my cap. Have you seen it? I can't find my

apron."

I thought that a twenty-something year old should be responsible for the attire and equipment that went with his job. I was struck and bewildered—those aren't strong enough words—to observe that my son, once capable of astutely juggling textbooks, notebooks, pencils, deadlines and intramural sports of high school, holding a part-time job, and wielding a clipboard and whistle to coach a young kids' basketball team to a championship, had regressed and become a husk of a person who could not manage to gather the three pieces of equipment needed for a dishwashing job. That it was my son behaving in this fashion was as inconceivable to me as inviting a stranger who doesn't value books to come in and rearrange my office.

I thought Matt's ineptness was a momentary glitch and he'd be back to his normal self soon. In the interim, well, some people might call my actions enabling. I took to gathering Matt's apron, shoes and cap and placing them together on a shelf, so he could find them quickly. I'd set the kitchen timer, so he'd know when to leave for work. And his car? Sometimes, while he slept in the mornings, I'd sneak his car to the gas station and put a half tank of gas in it, because I do not think he paid attention to the gauge. It was almost always on empty. I didn't want him to run out of gas on his way to work. I was always careful not to let the empty cigarette boxes that littered his car floor stir my worry into a boil.

Sure, I admit at my therapist's prompting, I was overinvolved. I want to glare at her and dare her to mention that I should, or could, have done differently.

It was easy for me to see that Steve was overinvolved in his own boisterous way. I wished he'd be different. One night, Carolyn invited two friends to sleep over and because Matt's bedroom was larger than hers, she convinced Matt to let them sleep in his bedroom. During the middle of the night, it started to pour. Steve woke me. "Hear that rain? I wonder if Matt's car's sunroof is open."

The previous day had been breezy and sunny. "Probably," I murmured. "He rarely shuts it."

"If it is, his car's interior will get soaked." Steve's words and tone spilled doom all over me. I just wanted to go back to sleep. Steve got up, went out into the downpour and ascertained that Matt's roof was, in fact, open. Coming back inside, Steve went into Carolyn's room and brusquely woke Matt, "Your sunroof is open."

Matt rustled under his blankets and turned to sink back to sleep.

"You need to get up and close your sunroof. It's pouring out."

Frustrated, that he couldn't rouse Matt, Steve yelled, "Why won't you take care of things? Where is your key?"

"In my room," Matt mumbled.

Steve stormed down the stairs to Matt's room, barged through the door, turned on the lights and bellowed to the sleeping girls, "Everybody up. We need to find a key."

By the time Steve closed the sunroof, the car's interior was soaked, and the rain was slowing. Carolyn was thoroughly embarrassed and declared that she wouldn't invite friends to sleep over ever again.

I often thought about our interactions with Matt. We wanted to change things for the better, but we lacked power. Usually all our exchanges—our suggestions, our imploring, begging and pleading, our constructive criticism, our scolding, our diatribes—increased the distance between all family members. From this (a few years later) vantage point, I think about enabling. I know now that a healthier practice would be to untangle, or disengage, from the unhealthy behavior. Once, I read that a bystander cannot force an individual into acting capably. The way to move forward is to stop helping. I couldn't stop helping. I worked diligently to keep our lives and relationships on their warped tack because I worried that if my efforts failed our lives would shred. And I was trying to protect Matt from Steve's anger. I was afraid that if I stopped my tinkering, my shell of a son would fade into nothingness and Steve would yell at me as it happened.

Chapter nine: Why are you like this?

Our valiant, but regularly thwarted, efforts to keep our family functioning often prompted interactions that seemed lifted from another family's script. We once enjoyed family togetherness and conversations, but things deteriorated until we didn't even know how to talk to each other. Once generous and truthful in our interactions. Now stingy and deceptive.

"We had a good visit," my mother declares when concluding phone calls, walks down Front Street and up past Ford's Lobster, or afternoons which culminate in dinner—baked scallops or fish—on my parent's deck with a view of boats gliding along the Mystic River. My mother uses the phrase "a good visit" often—either to declare that she's enjoyed one or to inquire as to whether I have had one. I think, in her opinion, an individual needs the comforts of home and a good visit to thrive.

To my mom, a good visit includes talk, lots of it. The talk doesn't have to touch on profound matters. It can be chatter about the weather—hurricanes past, a count of the number of sunny days in a row, the current direction of the wind and what that means for walkers and bikers. Food is a worthy topic. She welcomes a detailed description of what I ate for dinner or what I plan to prepare for tomorrow's dinner. Or better still, what she plans to cook for dinner. Best: what I'm going to cook or bake that she taught me to put together. Say I plan to try to replicate her prize-winning apple pie? She'll pass on tips. She'll share her tricks. My mom raised me to value good visits, good conversation, and good food.

I think it's my heritage to enjoy conversations that involve connecting in warm ways with people I've just met or people I've known a long time and like or love. I think that conversations are worth the effort of foraging for good topics to discuss and I like to think about asking questions to prompt people to tell more about their thoughts and feelings. I like a conversation that includes laughter and surprise. I value conversation during meals. I thought everyone did. However, years ago, as Steve and I prepared to sit down for our first dinner as a married couple, according to his family's practice, he turned the television on before pulling out his chair.

"No. That is not happening. If I make a dinner, we are not watching television while we eat." My preference slipped out and the strength of the words surprised even me. When I was growing up, there had been plenty of times that I had envied friends who were allowed to watch television while eating meals. However, as an adult the practice dismayed me, and, agreeably, Steve clicked the television off and over the years our practice became dinner and discussion.

I enjoy an interesting conversation, and I savor companionable silence. Sometimes, some places, experiencing silence with friends is like linking arms, or resting shoulder to shoulder, and letting a beauty that is too rich to describe with mere words spill over you.

But the awkward silence that became the norm for our dinners during Matt's depressed years was as uncomfortable as wearing a too-tight pair of itchy pants that shrunk as I wore them. We squirmed valiantly to bust out of the big squeeze of silence by commenting on weather, or our days, or the food.

I'd prepare dinner and announce it. We'd sit down. We'd bow our heads and pray. Aloud, Steve or I thanked God for the food. Silently, I pleaded for the ability to push back the unyielding, smothering silence.

After prayer, family members picked up their utensils and started to eat.

Sometimes, polite phrases like "pass the butter" or "pass

the salt, please" were murmured; however, I felt that actual conversation depended on me. I'd learned from my mom to chat about weather. So I'd pass the salt and pepper and say brightly, "Nice weather today!"

Steve might echo my thought and add an idea, "Yeah. The sun was nice."

Matt ate. He chewed. He swallowed. He dragged his fork or knife across the plate. Instead of fading into background noise, each act sounded loud, like a resounding gong, or a main event to gawk at.

I'd try to start another conversation, "So, I browned this chicken in olive oil."

Or I'd mention a news story. Or share something a student had said. Or a Penn State sports story. I felt like I was serving conversational delicacies when one of my students was a Penn State Athlete and I could share an inside scoop. "His three-point shot may help Penn State beat Michigan, but he sure doesn't care about commas."

Sometimes, Steve would get on a mission to compel Matt to respond.

"So Matt what do you think about that? What do you think about what your mother said?" My attempt to start a pleasant conversation became an interrogation in which one person angrily tried to badger the other into a response.

Matt stabbed a large piece of meat with his fork and shoved it in his mouth. He said nothing.

"Matt, your mother asked you a question. What is your answer?"

"I didn't ask Matt a question." I refused to join the mission to compel Matt. I was on the mission to coax Matt. There is a difference.

"I think you asked Matt a question." Steve scowled and slapped butter onto a slice of bread. "Matt needs to show respect and answer you."

And then we'd be talking about Matt in front of Matt. In heated tones. It was more wretched, and rude, than silence.

Matt remained as silent as concrete. We did not have good visits.

If the other kids—Carolyn and Phillip—were home,

conversation was a little easier. We'd talk in front and around and in spite of Matt. It was like playing catch while confined in a small room in which a sprawling concrete barrier hampered sight and action. And feeling that your very life depended on completion of the tosses.

Toss: "How was your day?"

Catch: "My day was good."

Toss: "Yours?"

We didn't say so, but we all wondered: do we toss to the silent person? Or do we toss and catch like he doesn't exist? It seemed awkward to ignore him. But we feared that if we prodded too much, instead of engaging, he'd retreat even further into himself.

The contrast between the conversationalist he had been growing up and the word-poor person he'd become was striking. When he was an only child, before our others were born, every evening he'd go to the kitchen for a snack and he'd call Steve and me to join. Seated between us, beaming with joy, he'd chatter. He mastered the essentials of a good visit as a child.

When he was in the depths of depression, we often gave in to silence, and I felt glad and grateful when Steve picked up the remote and turned on the television. Usually the news.

The conversations Matt and I did have were not over dinner and they often bewildered me.

Sometimes, I'd venture into Matt's bedroom and pick my way through the items of clothing that were strewn on the floor. I'd collect a half dozen coffee mugs that contained layers of colorful, swirling mold growing on a few swallows of coffee. "You need to clean up this room now."

He might move in the bed, pull his covers up higher and comment. "Mom, you just don't think about time the way I do. For me, time is..." and he would use words I knew to describe a sequence that made no sense. And, if I said honestly perplexed, "I have no idea what you are talking about.", he lashed out at me for not understanding.

Sometimes, he showed me a bump or a mark or an area of his skin, or the side of his stomach, and say, "I've been thinking about this bump. I think I have cancer. Do you see that?"

When I said I didn't see anything that merited concern, he growled at me and accused me of not caring. I learned to say, "Let's get a doctor's appointment."

While I watched, depression stole his healthy routine, his interests, his capabilities and our conversations. But I didn't realize I was observing a robbery in progress. I thought Matt chose to relinquish these treasures.

And then there were holidays.

During regular life, I don't dislike holidays, but I don't like them a whole lot. The pressure to manufacture an extra good time—prepare delicious food, surround myself with doting friends, wear festive clothes, initiate meaningful conversations, be inundated with warm emotion—intimidates me. It's just too much. I can tolerate the low-key holidays like Thanksgiving. It's the holidays with elaborate buildup and countdowns, like Christmas, that intimidate me.

"What are your holiday plans?" an interested friend's innocent question asked weeks before Christmas makes me feel muddled and inadequate. Should I already have plans?

The bar of holiday enjoyment is set higher than can be reached by our family with me planning the festivities, even in a good year. We can do the accepted routines. During the Christmas season, we haul a live tree into our house, set it up and argue about whether all white lights or multi-colored lights look better. We can hang beads and ornaments on the tree branches that stick out in irregular lengths and at slipshod angles. But to create a look that exudes charm or goodwill or a pleasing pattern is beyond our decorating capacity. Our tree is usually crammed into a corner of our smallish living room and scattered with haphazardly placed ornaments. We have collected the ornaments over the years—some purchased during after-Christmas sales, some created at ladies' craft nights, some handed down from my childhood, and some glued together by our kids—my favorite: a picture of six-year-old Carolyn, framed in a wreath made of green painted puzzle pieces. If our decorations were boxed and offered to a second-hand store, they'd be labelled junk and rejected.

We're not anti-holiday—we valiantly take a stab at participating in the accepted routines and the results underwhelm. In preparation for holidays, I have adjusted my outlook. Optimism pops within me that maybe this year the celebration magic will find us—the presents will satisfy, the food will be savored, the company and warm feelings will be sweet and enough. But I temper it. I want the rituals to ooze with sacred meaning and in the celebrating I want to touch life and to seal that impulse in our hearts. I am Charlie Brown forever returning to kick that football. But I catch myself. The hope of magic is a lie, I tell myself. And I resolve to face lame reality. And that's during a normal year.

During the years that Matt struggled so, holidays were even more challenging. I learned to brace for disappointment. I hunkered down and rode out the storm. I drew inward, muted hope and knew the holidays would pass.

I remember one Christmas season vividly. The day we went to cut the Christmas tree, Matt actually got out of bed to go with us. I almost seem to recall that he spearheaded the excursion. Steve and I were operating in a sad daze, content to let Christmas slip by without physical evidence of the season in our home, but Matt insisted on setting up a tree. I could be wrong. I do know that during the selection process, Matt expressed an opinion of more than three words. And we went with it. When we arrived home, Matt dragged the tree inside, singlehandedly, and set it in its stand. A few days later, Matt had purchased, wrapped and set a present or two under the tree. However, by the actual day of Christmas, he had expended all his energy. On Christmas day, he declined to get out of bed.

On Christmas morning, a light coating of snow meant Steve was called in to work to tend to road conditions. There were presents under the tree, but Steve didn't want us to open them until he got home. Phillip, Carolyn and I couldn't lure Matt out of bed for breakfast. Our extended family was out of town. My neighbor, knowing the kids and I were home alone, invited us over, to join their family celebration. So at least Carolyn and I, and maybe Phillip, went to the neighbor's and tried to participate. We overheard conversations and participated in some. We ate some good food. But knowing that Matt wouldn't get out of bed on Christmas Day was the only thing I could think of. I tried to have a good visit, to politely converse, but it was like the message was written in strobe lights and flashing again and again in my mind: My son is home in bed on Christmas Day. Our family cannot celebrate because one of our members will not get out of bed.

I felt so sad.

When Steve came home from work, I offered him a plate of food that I'd carried from the neighbor's and we tried to enjoy some family time. But Matt wouldn't get out of bed. Steve didn't act sad. He fumed. And the thing I remember most about that Christmas Day was Steve's frustration. He yelled at Matt, "Why are you like this? What is wrong with you?"

Matt got up for a short time. We unwrapped gifts. We said words like, "how nice" and "just what I wanted" and "thank you"—but they were hollow words. They didn't mean anything. Generosity and gratitude and joy had been stamped out.

I decided I needed to get away. The weather was okay for travel, so I quickly made plans to take Carolyn and drive to visit my parents in New England.

Matt went back to bed. I sat beside him, softly stroking his head with my fingers. Tears slipped from his eyes. "I don't know what to do, Mom."

I wish I had known to say: depression is a disease and we are going to get you the medical help you need. Right now.

It was sometime later. Maybe a few weeks. Maybe a few months. Maybe even a year, or more. I picked up a magazine that featured an article on depression. I can remember clearly the exact spot in the room where I stood when the story's title caught my eye. I could go stand there right now, if you wanted. I paged to the article on depression. In my mind's eye, I can still see the artwork. The page featured a gray, shadowy shape—an indistinct outline of a slumped person.

I scanned the text and read: Depression is a disease. That some people are genetically predisposed to.

I read the symptoms: persistent feelings of sadness; loss of energy; loss of interests; fatigue; slowing of physical processes, including thought processes; substance abuse and irritability. Call me master detective Sherlock Holmes. I began to suspect that Matt suffered from a very severe case of depression. Eventually, Steve and I learned that expecting severely depressed Matt to get out of bed to celebrate Christmas was like asking a person with two broken legs and fear of water to run a 5k that culminated in a polar bear plunge.

We counted on Matt to perform a physical impossibility. He couldn't. He needed medical help. I loudly cheered him on, not realizing I was saying again and again, "Do the impossible." When he didn't, I silently blamed myself, blamed Steve and blamed Matt.

He was not a participant in this grand theft, but an injured victim, left to flounder and squirm. One thing I've learned to say loudly is that people with mental illness like clinical depression need medical help.

But I'm getting ahead of my story.

That Christmas Day I asked Matt, "Do you want to come with Carolyn and me to Grandma and Grandpa's?"

My mother was good with Matt. If anyone could get him out of bed for a few days in a row, she could. She's got energy and words, and so much love.

"Yes."

"We are going to leave early in the morning. You'll have to get out of bed. Early. By eight o'clock."

He came. He slept hours upon hours at my parents. Now and then, he got up to walk by the water and secretly smoke a cigarette.

When he'd return from his walk, my mother would ask, "Does he smoke?"

"He says he doesn't."

Chapter ten: Ill-equipped people

Once, I counted and realized that Matt had been fired from more than eight jobs over the years. He'd been fired for a variety of reasons:

1. He'd grown his hair to shoulder length and refused to cut it when the restaurant manager asked him to.
2. He was late to work. Repeatedly.
3. He stole alcohol from the restaurant.
4. He showed up to work reeking of alcohol.
5. He got stuck in Haiti in a demonstration and couldn't get a flight back for two days. He couldn't alert his boss because he didn't have the workplace phone number with him in Haiti.
6. He got confused about a work schedule and didn't show up for a scheduled shift.
7. He made a costly mistake with the equipment.
8. He didn't get along with the boss's son.

Matt could always find a job and work for a while, but after a few weeks something would happen, and the job would end. For many years, Matt couldn't hold a job.

The first firing, the one prompted by the newly grown, shoulder-length hair, Matt knew that was coming. He was warned. The job required washing dishes at a local restaurant. He'd held the job through two, maybe three, years of high school and then he decided to grow his hair long. The manager objected and threatened to let him go, but Matt claimed, "She won't fire me. I'm the best dishwasher in the place." I think his self-assessment of his work was accurate. At that time, he worked fast and efficiently. I wasn't a fan of his long hair but didn't see how she could fire him for it as long as he wore a hairnet. Girls that worked there that had long hair. Did she order them to get their hair cut?

I think Matt kept forgetting—or omitting, maybe intentionally—to wear the hairnet.

After he was let go, Matt angrily sputtered a phrase from a song he liked, "longhaired hippie kids need not apply." He seemed to believe the restaurant manager had unfairly slighted him and that by keeping his hair long he was standing for a cause. I told him that he was cutting off his nose to spite his face. He ignored my comment and continued to grow his hair. At the time, I didn't favor his stance, but in the years that followed, when he rarely talked, I often wished that he'd stand up and stake a claim. Any claim. Even for shoulder-length hair. I longed for him to express an opinion.

Matt seemed to brush off the firing, but I smarted. My son being let go was like a scrape on my soul. I know mothers of fired kids are not branded in neon, but I felt ashamed and I thought the shame was as visible as if I were branded with a bright, flashing sign that blinked: "Failure."

I could so see the second firing coming. Matt had quit college for the first time, and somehow landed a decent job with decent pay at a furniture store. The work was not strenuous. He liked the people he worked with. But still he struggled every morning to get out of bed. He'd leave for work late. Regularly, he was fifteen to twenty minutes late to work. I warned him, "You better get there on time."

"They don't care. All they do is sit around and drink coffee for the first thirty minutes, or so."

"Believe me, they care."

"No. If they cared they'd say something."

I couldn't convince him that turning up for work on time was one of the unspoken requirements of a diligent worker. One day, he left for work, and an hour later he returned, looking more grim than usual.

"He fired me. He didn't even say why," Matt griped.

I told him why. But he didn't believe me. He concluded that he'd been doomed from the start. That the boss just didn't like him.

Again, I felt shame. Like I had messed up. I thought I'd taught my kids important life lessons like diligence in work. But Matt didn't seem to recall or, at least, believe the lessons. His approach to life meant he'd have to learn things by doing what he wanted and then suffering the consequences. It seemed like a difficult way to learn and made me flinch. I wondered if I was responsible for his pain. Should I have worked harder or differently to make sure he understood how life worked?

Each time, after losing a job, Matt spent mornings (if he got up) avidly reading the want ads in the paper.

Steve insisted on an intense job search and tried to prompt it by stabbing the air with his index finger and directing terse commands at Matt, "You need a job." Or at me, "He needs a job. —He needs a forty-hour-a-week job."

And Matt tried, but never as diligently as Steve desired. Steve wanted Matt to spend eight hours a day, five or six days a week, looking. Many days, Steve called me from work at regular intervals to press me to press Matt to job hunt.

"And how is this going to look on his resume?" Steve groaned. He'd get face to face with Matt and say again and again that when employers looked at resumes, they considered how many jobs a person has held in the past and having a lot of jobs for a short time is not a plus. It's a minus. A huge minus. "An employer's going to ask, 'why did you leave that job?' You'll have to explain."

Steve glared at me. "He'll have to explain."

I knew the resume advice was accurate. People in our culture need resumes to obtain jobs, to succeed in life. But when facing our challenges, I didn't think that far ahead. I concentrated on slogging through the next few hours. And I focused intently on avoiding Steve's anger which seemed directed at me because I had somehow failed at making sure Matt kept his job.

Sometimes, I almost welcomed the job-hunting challenge because it provided a focus, so we wouldn't have to consider the problem that we lived with but couldn't identify.

On the surface, Matt seemed to consider the repeated firings as trifling and annoying, like gnats to evade or swat away. However, I think the occurrences began to take their toll and Matt slipped deeper and deeper into grim limbo and the belief that he didn't have skills to offer in the workplace.

Most of the firings resulted from his actions. It's not fun to watch a son suffer the consequences of his own actions but knowing that he's getting what he deserves is a way to make sense of the circumstances. Most the time I knew that Matt deserved to be fired.

Even so, each firing diminished him. His drive to succeed was depleted. His confidence that he could meet work expectations drained.

During the spring of 2011, due to legal reasons, which I'll talk about in detail later, Matt did not have a driver's license. He had floundered for a lot of years. Losing his license was another failure—and he lost it more than once—that added to his feelings of ineptness. We live too far from town to access public transportation. Without his license, Matt biked some places and relied on me to drive him others. When driving him, I tried to pour kindness into him. That spring, when I picked him up from work, I often arrived with a delicious iced coffee drink. I wanted him to know that life could be hard, jobs could be mundane, but when we work diligently, we can treat ourselves. Treating myself at regular intervals is one of the practices I use to keep myself going through life's hard parts.

At the time, Matt worked painting apartments. He didn't really like the work, but it provided two things he needed: money and a schedule. Each morning, I woke him up, coerced him out of bed (I'd promise coffee, or bacon for breakfast, or, when I got really desperate, I'd throw ice and water on him) and drove him to work. Eight hours later, on the way to pick him up, I hoped fervently that he'd be in the spot where we'd agreed to meet and that he was still employed. Neither was a given.

At that time in his life, Matt did not express desire for anything—I'd ask him what he wanted to eat for a meal or snack and he'd murmur a low, "Whatever." I'd invite him to go somewhere and he'd decline and go to bed, pulling the covers up over his head and turning to face the wall. When he arranged a week off from his job to travel with our family to Haiti and work, as part of a team, painting buildings, building a tilapia farm, surfacing a basketball court and enjoying time with the orphanage kids, I was surprised.

I was nervous about Matt coming on the trip because visiting Haiti is a many-faceted challenge. Emotionally healthy people find visiting Haiti disconcerting. While I find visiting Haiti intriguing, and sometimes delightful, the experience is also jarring. The scorching sun and heat pierce my body and wring out the strength. People talk loudly in a language I don't understand, press into my personal space and vie to carry my luggage for a dollar or two or beg me to buy their artwork, "Please, Mum. Please. My work is good." Or they plead, "I'm hungry. I haven't eaten in three days. Please, Mum. Give me food. Please."

I see signs that I don't understand or signs that I do understand but are puzzling, like the message repeatedly stamped on a concrete wall surrounding a compound: No trespassing risk to be molested and put in jail.

When our bus threads a narrow way through a jumble of dented, honking cars, I usually feel like I've been dropped into chaos.

As we ride through the city of Port-au-Prince to our destination, we see houses that range in quality. Some are awkward structures of tarps, cardboard and corrugated steel laced haphazardly together. Others are gated, sprawling structures of colorfully painted stucco. Many are unfinished, but lived-in, and rebar in varying heights sticks out of the first story roofs. I've been told the homes are deliberately left unfinished because occupants don't have to pay taxes until the home is completed.

We see people in a range of clothing. Some are smartly dressed in business suits and they stride with purpose through the crowds. Some ride motorcycles with three to four individuals squeezed and straddling a bike. None wear helmets. Some people are semi-clothed or naked and they squat by foul-smelling, murky streams washing themselves or scrubbing clothes.

I see barefooted kids skillfully dribbling and passing a soccer ball while a skinny cow ambles across the play space. The cow stops to pull a green weed from the packed dirt and stands munching. The kid with the ball dribbles around and kicks the ball through the gap between two stones, scoring a goal. Nearby, men seated at a card table in the shade of a tree concentrate intensely on dominos.

One of my favorite life moments happened on a Haitian beach at a resort. Along with Carolyn and Steve and a couple of friends, I was sunning myself on a plastic lounge chair and a skinny man with leathery skin paddled a roughhewn wooden kayak to the shore. He unfolded from his seat and stepped on the sand carrying a netted bag full of coconuts and an ancient looking machete. He picked a coconut from his bag, loped off the end and handed the coconut to me indicating I should drink the milk. My friends and I took turns slurping milk from that giant coconut. It tasted so good. The juice dribbled down our chins. The experience seemed so exotic. I felt like I was enjoying communion at the juncture of ancient and modern.

When I am in Haiti, the stark contrasts hold my attention. Sometimes, they are beautiful. Sometimes, ugly. The contrast between what I think is the bare minimum access to physical comfort for a normal life and what I see makes me flinch. To me, many scenes scream with pain and need. And it seems like I'm in a horror film where the villain destroys lives and inflicts pain and the good guys smile and do one small defensive maneuver, maybe, when they are not too hot, but mostly they smile and make way for the villain to destroy innocent people.

We are advised not to walk alone in the streets, be out after dark, drink the water, or eat the food unless it's prepared for Americans.

A trip to Haiti would challenge Matt in many ways, and I worried it would cause him excessive mental stress, but he wanted to go. In the weeks leading up to the trip, I tried valiantly to equip him for the discomforts he would face. The group we traveled with provided all our necessary items—like food and water. But they didn't provide cigarettes. He was a smoker then and smoked at least a half a pack a day.

I didn't like to facilitate smoking, but I didn't think Matt could cope with the agitation of uncomfortable surroundings and going without cigarettes. "I don't know where you can buy cigarettes in Haiti, so bring a carton." I instructed. I even drove him to a convenience store, so he could buy the carton. While I sat in the car, he went into the store and came back out. Then, I drove him to the bank to cash his check. "Get cash in ones and fives. We'll be in a small village where you can't use a bill that is larger than a five." He went into the bank and came back out. He claimed he was ready for Haiti, but I feel like no one is ever ready for Haiti.

On the morning of the first full day, along with other members of our crew, we climbed into the bed of a pickup truck for the ride from our lodging to an orphanage. A couple of people shared seats on inside wheel fenders. Some perched on the truck bed walls and some sat cross-legged on the truck bed floor. Others, who'd sat on the end of the truck bed with their feet dangling, pulled their legs up awkwardly when the driver insisted on slamming the tail gate.

The truck moved slowly along a dusty, rutted, narrow roadway dodging makeshift market booths, goats, and skinny dogs. The driver honked the horn loudly and at regular intervals to alert people that we were coming through. Grim-faced people edged out of the way. To avoid pot-holes large enough to swallow two tires, the driver turned sharply and frequently. Passengers braced to stay in position but with each swerve, we teetered, swayed and slid heavily into each other until the next turn when we toppled another way. Some giggled nervously. I hooked my arm over the truck bed's wall to steady and plant myself. I looked across the tangle of people at Matt and wondered how he felt. He hadn't been in a confined space this physically close to people in a long time.

We rode past homes and places of business—makeshift shelters with corrugated metal roofs supported by crooked, skinny branches. Garbage and litter lay on the ground; sometimes in heaps. In one heap, a goat feeding on scraps had stuck its hoof through the lid of a cardboard box. And now the goat wore the box like a cumbersome, rectangle shackle. The people we passed called out "blanc" which means white and some called out another phrase which our guide refused to interpret. He seemed embarrassed to tell us. But eventually, we coaxed him into revealing they hollered out, "Greedy!"

Children ran behind chattering and pointing. "Can we throw them candy?" One member of the team wanted to demonstrate that we were not greedy.

We stopped at a modern looking gas station and negotiated the price for a bag of ice in which to store our bottled water. "Don't put the ice in your mouths," we were warned.

I pulled my hand sanitizer from my bag and rubbed it over my hands.

Eventually, we pulled through metal gates onto the orphanage grounds. Inside the fenced-in compound, each team member was assigned a task and provided with limited tools and limited supplies. My task was to paint the outside walls of one of the buildings. The orphanage kids wanted to help, so over the next few hours, without knowing their language, I shared my limited knowledge of how to paint, refereed scuffles over whose turn it was to use the one good paint brush, insisted they keep the paint in the cans and off their clothes, plus do a decent-looking job. My stomach growled. I was hot and tired, but compelled by a desire to finish the task, I worked harder. My head swam. The available iced water was in a cooler way across the dusty orphanage grounds—the desert, we called it—so I drank some lukewarm water which was almost certainly clean. Kids eager to help tried to use dead leaves or twigs or other makeshift tools to apply paint to the walls. I distracted them. A bee stung me. I really wanted a piece of ice to ease the sting. I looked for shade to sit in and plopped my bottom in the dirt. I looked up and saw Matt trudging across the dusty compound towards me. He had a white tea towel draped over his head. His face was beet red. Sweat beaded on the outside of his water bottle. Maybe his water was cold. I reached for it. He handed it to me. I gulped a swig of cold water.

"Mom, where's the nearest ATM machine?"

In that season of our lives, no matter how annoyed or panicked I felt, I always tempered my responses to him. I opted for calm and gentle. I thought that an angry or incredulous reaction might push his fragile emotions to a breaking point, and I didn't want him to break. But that day, I felt hot, tired and pushed to the limits of caring.

"ATM machine? Did you see one on the way here? Back by that goat in the trash heap maybe?" I blurted.

Matt wiped his sweaty forehead, streaking it gray with his dirty hand. "I need some cash. I need to buy a cigarette."

"I thought you brought cigarettes." Maybe he'd left them at the hotel.

"No. I didn't want to buy a carton. It was too expensive. I thought I'd quit while I was here."

I stretched my hand out, so he could pull me up. "I have no idea where you can get a cigarette." I took the corner of the damp towel that he'd draped over his head and wiped a gray streak on his forehead.

"I can get one. There's a guy down the road who sells stuff. I just need some cash."

"Use the fives and ones you brought."

"I didn't bring any. I figured I'd just use the ATM."

My fives and ones were back at our accommodations. I don't know if I'd have given him any cash if I'd had it. There is a limit to the lengths that I will go to rescue my children.

And that was the theme of that chapter of our lives—how far would I go to equip him? I tried so hard to prepare him for the situations he'd encounter, but he'd often refuse to co-operate.

Somehow, he got cigarettes that trip. He smoked outside the orphanage grounds, careful not to let the kids see him.

I was nervous about the kids seeing him smoking. I was nervous about him being outside the orphanage grounds by himself.

When he worked, he worked diligently. When he rested, he'd sit in silence and the little kids would crawl onto his lap. He'd awkwardly pat their shoulders or rub their backs. He was ill-equipped, but he survived.

And maybe that is the point of my story, the sum of what I have to tell. We are ill-equipped people. To thrive, to help our loved ones learn to live with mental illness, we must identify and obtain the right tools. That's hard to do in the middle of crisis—but it's imperative.

There is one main road from the hotel to the Port-au-Prince airport and on the day of our departure, on our way back to the city, we were stopped in a demonstration. We were passengers in the bed of a truck. The bed was enclosed with a metal cage. We called it the cage truck. We might have been white folk paraded on display.

Through the metal screen, we could see burning tires blocking the road ahead. A crowd of excited, yelling people milled around the tires. Our translator learned that in the village we were approaching, a large tractor trailer truck was intentionally parked across the road to keep traffic from moving through. We heard gunshots in the distance. "They are shooting in air," explained an English-speaking bystander.

"If you walk, they'll let you through," said another. "They aren't upset with you. They know you've come to help."

"They are protesting because they want electricity," said someone else.

I pictured the group of us, with our suitcases rolling behind, walking through the smoke and volatile crowd without shared language to explain our trek. And what would we do on the other side? We turned around and missed our flight home. We couldn't book another for two days.

Matt didn't have his work phone number with him and couldn't call work to report the delay. When, back in the United States, he reappeared at work a few days later than expected the boss said he was no longer needed.

"It's his fault," Steve said. "He should've called them."

I could completely understand not bringing a phone number to Haiti where we didn't have phone service anyway. But calling in when you can't show up is one of the basics of keeping a job. Matt was fired again.

I was glad about one letting go; it wasn't exactly a firing. Matt had landed a roofing job. The crew was stripping shingles off a roof that was more than two stories high. It might have been five. Matt didn't often ever tell me about his workday, but one day he said to me, "I almost fell off the roof today."

"Don't they strap you in? What kind of safety equipment are you using?"

Matt didn't answer. I wanted him to quit the job but knew that act wouldn't add substance to his resume, so I didn't voice my wish. I was glad when the roof was finished and Matt said the boss would call when he had another job. The phone didn't ring and if the roofing number had showed up on caller ID, I might not have picked up.

Most the time we learned from Matt that he lost a job. Once we got a call from the boss who told Steve he'd fired Matt for stealing alcohol. Absorbing his message, I felt like I'd been sucked into a tornado of despair and I couldn't perceive a way out. I sat on the steps, with my head in my hands, listening for Matt's car to pull into the driveway. He didn't come home for a long time.

The only time I don't like hearing Matt's car pull into the driveway is when I know it's way too early to be home from work.

I knew the sum of all these lost jobs must be enormous and it couldn't be positive. It wasn't until I read a confidential message written by Matt's doctor to a judge that things became clearer.

Chapter eleven: Breathe in, breathe out

I began to suspect that Matt was driving drunk and I mentioned my concern to him.

"Are you driving drunk?"

"Nope."

His response did not flood me with relief. I wanted his denial to ring true, but it didn't. I tried another approach. I delivered a well-timed mini sermon. (You know how effectively sermons work to motivate). "Drunk driving can result in all kinds of terrible unintended mishaps like terrible accidents and deaths. I don't want you to die. Or cause someone else do die."

"Me, either."

"You'd never drive drunk. Would you?" I tried to make eye contact with him. To see into his soul. Or at least gauge the sincerity of his response.

"Nope." He turned his back and left the room. I think that "Nope" meant "Leave me alone."

I don't recall exactly why I suspected Matt was driving drunk. Maybe the empty beer bottles I found hidden around the house. Behind the couch. Under Matt's bed. The whiskey bottle that was hidden in the basement behind the freezer.

I respect somewhat my grown kids' rights to privacy. I don't open their mail or snoop, too much, in their rooms. Since Matt had saved the money and purchased his own car I didn't feel right rooting through the junk in the back seat, but once I peeked in the window and saw empty beer cans lying on the floor.

I cornered him. "You know there are laws against drinking and driving. Like you can't have open containers of alcohol in your car. That's against the law. You know that, right?"

"Yup."

"And the open, empty beer cans that are on the floor in the back seat of your car?"

"Not mine."

Breathe in. Breathe out.

I suppose that there is a scenario in which those empties were not his. Maybe he, Matt, noticed empty beer cans lying on the roadside and concern about the environmental impact of litter compelled him to pick them up. There is a time and a place in which he could have done that. We actually participated in litter pickups on our road when he was a kid. I suppose that some remnant of stewardship might stir him to see litter, stop, pick it up and toss it in his back seat. I suppose in a galaxy far, far away mothers don't worry about their kids or try to steer outcomes for their kids' maximum benefit, or at least for their safety. (I didn't worry about Matt thriving. I worried about keeping him and others alive.)

My attention had shrunk to a narrow focus. I had two reasons for worry. When Matt was home in his bed, I worried about how to get him out of bed. When Matt drove off in his car, I worried about him driving and drinking.

In bed, I'd lay awake at night and listen for him to arrive home from his dishwashing job. I knew the job ended about midnight. The drive from the restaurant to our home was short. But the wait, until one or two o'clock when I heard the crunch of his tires on our driveway, was long. Sometimes, he'd arrive home, come in, shower and leave again. In the dark, flat on my back, pillows adjusted, I listened alertly for the second crunch of his tires. It was the signal to ratchet up the worry.

Of course, I prayed. I tried to exchange my worry for prayer—with varying degrees of success.

In summer, if Matt didn't leave home after his shower, he sat on the porch smoking. The smoke wafted up and the fan in our window pulled the smoke into our bedroom. Steve would wake up, throw back the covers, get out of bed, and yell, "Stop smoking outside our window. Some of us have to work in the morning."

"He's smoking on the porch," Steve would tell me.

I wanted to say, "That's a good thing. If he's on the porch, then he's not driving drunk."

However, Steve and I argued about so much already. I didn't want to add any more fuel to that fire. I didn't know for sure that Matt was mixing driving and drinking.

One evening, Matt drove in as usual. He showered. He left the house. I heard his car door slam, but I didn't hear the car start.

I got out of bed, pushed the shade to the side, peered out my bedroom window and saw him sitting in his car in the driveway. I wrapped a robe around me, stuck my feet into slippers, walked down the stairs and outside to the passenger door. I tapped on the window.

"Let me in."

"What do you want? Go to bed."

"I just want to talk."

"I don't want to talk," he said but he unlocked the door.

I climbed into the smoke-filled car. The driver's side window was open about two inches. He held a lit cigarette through the gap. We sat in silence for a long time. A couple times, he put the cigarette to his mouth and sucked on it. And then he'd exhale smoke. I tried to make small talk. I asked about his evening at work.

It was like approaching a wounded victim who is lying broken and bleeding in a field of debris and asking, "So how was your day?"

He said nothing. So it was worse than approaching a disaster victim. If you came across a silent, mutilated victim you could perform a rescue.

I tried another approach.

"You didn't leave the driveway tonight, but usually you go somewhere."

He grunted. "Yeah."

"Are you planning to leave now?"

"Why do you care?"

"I'm afraid you're driving drunk."

"I don't drive drunk."

"You don't smoke, either."

He had told me again and again that he didn't smoke. When I'd point out his need for cigarettes' in Haiti or the cigarette butt pile that had accumulated in the mulch off the porch, he'd mumble. "Yeah, but I quit."

Did he think that if he said what I wanted to hear I wouldn't nag? That words would placate or distract me when any fool could see that he was destroying his own life?

I knew I couldn't trust his claims.

(Once, years later, he told me that he'd drive to a church parking lot and drink a six-pack and smoke and think. He didn't drink while driving. He drank and then drove.)

Sometimes, I voiced my concerns to Steve. Once, he went out and pulled an empty plastic whiskey bottle from the back seat and hurled it across the driveway at Matt. "This needs to stop."

Steve and I thought Matt was choosing this danger that was rising up to destroy him. I felt helpless to rescue him. Steve felt angry. Steve felt like a failure as a dad. He told me that he often worried, "What did I do wrong that my son acts like this?"—We labeled Matt's actions as rebellious and foolish.

The morning after my talk with Matt in his car, I sat at the kitchen table and cried and prayed, "What do I do?"

I decided to call the police, thinking that maybe they'd have a suggestion. A fix. I looked up the telephone number in a telephone book and prepared to dial. I hoped I wouldn't have to talk too much because saying too many words might stir up the sobs which I squelched on a regular basis. I didn't want to cry on the phone. I tried to sound matter of fact. Like I wasn't calling about a matter of life and death. It seemed like hiding my desperation was the only way to slog through a day. I bit the inside of my cheeks. I braced my insides. I said the words calmly and slowly, "I think my son is driving drunk." Breathe in. Breathe out.

It was the first time I had said the words aloud. The admission launched an avalanche of emotion. I felt fear. I felt shame. I felt hope because I was reaching for help. "I don't know for sure, but I suspect and I don't know what to do. Is there a class I could insist he take? Or that we could take together?"

"I don't know of a class. I could come out and arrest him."

"Arrest?" I suspected that included handcuffs and court and jail. "That's one of the things I'm hoping he avoids. Is there anything else?" Was I the first mother to call with this need?

"Just let me know where you live, when you suspect that he's driving drunk and I'll come out and arrest him." He might as well have suggested that I cut my child in pieces and feed him to piranhas.

I hadn't given him my name yet. Would he try to trace the call? Would he come anyway? I was silent a long time. I willed him to come up with another alternative.

"I tell you what I do," he said. "Whenever there's a news report of drunk driving—an accident, someone hurt or killed, I read the story to my kids. I show them the newspaper. They know not to drive drunk."

I was familiar with his attitude. Once, I had flaunted the same confidence. I never said so to a mother who was ashamed and fearful regarding her kid's behavior, but I knew right from wrong and worked hard to ingrain that knowledge in my kids. My God, what mother doesn't teach her kids to avoid drinking and driving?

"How old are your kids?" I eventually asked.

"Ten and eight."

At age ten and age eight, my son, a D.A.R.E. graduate, knew not to drive drunk, I thought. But I didn't say so.

Here's what I want to say to you parents who are reading: it's not your fault. Mental illness is a disease that can impact anyone. Sometimes, substance abuse is a symptom of that disease.

After my conversation with the policeman, I hung up the phone and paged through the yellow pages looking for help.

I found an organization that advertised counseling for troubled teens and their families. I called and explained our situation. "We need help. Our family needs help." I said in squeaks mixed with sobs. The woman I talked to listened patiently and kindly and she said they could help. She scheduled us for an appointment with a psychologist who was adept at helping families in situations like ours. I had thought we were the only ones. I didn't want anyone else to feel this pain, but hearing there were other families that struggled helped me feel, for a moment, less alone. I marked the date for the scheduled appointment on the calendar. I counted the weeks—three. Could we avert catastrophe that long? I resolved to keep breathing. Breathe in. Breathe out. Breathe in.

Chapter twelve: Not about drinking

We made it without catastrophe to that Monday appointment. Steve, Matt and I sat in the lobby of the psychologist's office. We filled out paperwork and provided insurance cards and sat in awkward silence—the three of us—waiting. At intervals, Steve or Matt got up to roam the waiting room. Eventually, the doctor called us into his office. I'm not going to call him by his real name because what I have to say won't enhance his reputation. I'll call him Dr. Windbag.

He was a large man with a large, protruding belly and a jocular manner that contrasted with my desperate feelings and grated on me. He told a few jokes aimed at making Matt smile. He didn't care if Steve and I thought his material was funny. We didn't. Matt looked impassive. Maybe slightly impressed that Doctor catered to him—believe me, Matt noticed. Eventually, the doctor asked for our story. Steve talked. Matt responded in a few words. They were both angry and spewed resentment.

I piped up. "They really love each other. They have loved each other for a long time, but recently, they've been having heated disagreements."

They didn't sound like they ever remembered loving each other.

The doctor listened and then began to talk. He regaled himself with stories of his youth and his high school football career and his dabbling in drinking alcohol—even though his parents didn't understand.

I was dismayed that we were paying to listen Dr. Windbag's soliloquy that impressed only him. I thought we were paying to have the hour be focused on us. He changed his tack and spoke of kids stretching boundaries and stated that drinking was a normal part of adolescence for some kids.

"But we—I—think he's driving drunk," I blurted.

He turned to Matt and schmoozed about the importance of being truthful in the space of the office and declared that no one who was truthful in the space of the office would get in trouble with parents or police for admitting that they were driving drunk and there'd be no repercussions if a person (Matt) admitted to driving drunk. "You drink? With your buddies?"

"Yeah," Matt said.

I pictured the empty alcohol bottles in his car and the two empties I'd found behind the couch that morning. I hadn't told Steve. Yet.

"You drive drunk? While drinking?"

"Nope." Matt said.

Our hour was up. That was the end of session number one.

A week later, session number two was for Matt alone. I made sure he got there.

A week after that, session number three was Steve and I alone. "Your son is behaving like other kids his age. His behavior is normal. We can work through this. Tell me about your opinion of drinking alcohol."

Although I drink an occasional glass of wine or bottle of beer, I don't much like alcohol. I can take it or leave it. Although Steve drinks a beer or two more often than I do, his opinion is similar. I didn't experiment with alcohol as a kid. Steve did.

The doctor stated that our narrow view of alcohol's place in life was the problem and he told me that Matt wouldn't have to hide his drinking if we relaxed our control. I don't often like to be told that I'm wrong or to pay money to be told that I'm wrong. But I liked this message. I wanted to hear that my son's behavior was normal. I wanted to know that the empties I found under the couch, under his bed, behind the freezer in the basement did not indicate a problem.

So early in our journey, two professionals who deal with troubled people on a regular basis (the policeman who had arrested Matt for trespassing and this psychologist) stated that Matt's behavior was within the range of normal.

Did I need to readjust my perspective of normal?

I wanted to.

But something inside me remained on high alert. And since, I've learned to trust my mother's sense.

Chapter thirteen: Baby Steps

Probably all three of us would have remained stuck, pinned in a small, unhappy existence, plagued by despair and inactivity, slouching our way to death, but Matt and Steve regularly set each other on edge—their interactions, in which Matt was mostly silent, were steeped in hostility. My declarations of their love for each other and the doctor's claims that Matt's behavior was normal teenage stretching of limits didn't change their dynamics. They needed to live in separate houses.

We learned of an open house at the Pennsylvania College of Technology which is a college related to Penn State where Matt could go on discounted tuition because of my job. Although Matt didn't clearly embrace further education as a goal, he and Steve planned a college visit which included attending a basketball game. We thought that Matt could go to the school and, possibly, play on the basketball team.

The scenario felt like such a possibility to me. Like we'd been trapped in a cramped, dark space and then I glimpsed a way out, a way to spring from the shackles and gain freedom. The school offered majors in areas that had once interested Matt. The basketball team might be an opportunity. He could try out. He once had the skills and the interest in playing basketball. Maybe they could be reignited. The chance that he could play was reasonable.

The day that Steve and Matt traveled to visit the school, we traded vehicles. They took the car that I usually drove.

Around dinner time, Carolyn, Phillip and I climbed in Steve's truck and headed out for pizza. The outing was a meager attempt to have our lives not be all about Matt. We were doing something fun on a school night.

An unexpected, light snow coated the roads. I wasn't accustomed to driving the truck and couldn't crest a hill. It was a small hill. But the truck tires spun on the slippery road and I couldn't gain the traction to ease forward. When I gassed it, the rear tires shifted precariously. I had to cautiously back down the narrow road, careful not to hit any cars coming up. I was nervous about slipping into the other lane in front of an oncoming car.

We headed home without a pizza.

An uneasy dread enveloped me. I worried that our aborted pizza excursion was an omen. That it meant Matt and Steve's trip would not go well and that attending this school was not the step forward I hoped for. I reminded myself that I didn't believe in omens. I believed in the God who'd said to me that my prayer for my son had been answered. I believed God was at work in Matt's life. Things would be fine.

I went to bed before Steve and Matt got home, but the next morning at breakfast, I felt relieved when Steve declared the trip more success than not. Matt was interested in going to school and set to apply.

Steve left for work. I prepared to head to my sister's to exercise. We often exercised together in her exercise room. As I poured a cup of coffee to take with me, Matt appeared in the kitchen. "You're up early," I noted.

"I'm taking the dog and going to cut wood."

"What?"

"I'm taking the dog and going back in the woods to cut firewood."

Sometimes, he and Steve sawed up downed trees into firewood to use in our wood stove, but usually they did it together. Matt's plans seemed unusual. I asked, "How did your trip go?"

I don't recall his answer, but something didn't feel right. Matt seemed on edge. When I look back, it seems I recognized a trace of hysteria in his manner, but maybe not.

Matt headed with a pickup truck to the woods. I headed to my sister's. We were exercising when her landline phone began to ring repeatedly. We ignored the ring, but the caller kept calling and finally we paused our workout, so she could answer the phone. I heard her side of the conversation.

"Hello?"

"She's here."

"He's what?"

"Where is he now?"

"What do you want her to do?"

I don't remember if my sister relayed the news to me or if I got on the phone and Steve told me, but the report that interrupted our exercise session was that our family was no longer perched on the brink of a drunk-driving arrest. We'd toppled into that disaster. At nine thirty that morning, Matt had been arrested for driving drunk. And during the arrest, he was belligerent with the police officers. He might be charged with resisting arrest. When he was released, and Steve picked him up at the station he was hostile and rude.

Disoriented and almost dizzy, I paced restlessly in my sister's kitchen. I sat down. I got up and moved to another chair. My stomach felt queasy. I'd expected disaster, and I'd tried to prevent it, but in the moment of crisis, I hadn't recognized imminent danger and now I didn't know if there was life after a drunk-driving arrest.

Turns out, there is. But not with Dr. Windbag as facilitator.

When, at our next session, we told him about the arrest, he rubbed his chin, stared off in the distance, picked up a pen, wrote a name on a slip of paper and handed it to us, saying, "I thought that Matt was just engaged of normal age-appropriate drinking behavior. I guess not. Here's the name of a psychiatrist he should see."

"Do we reschedule with you?"

"See what the psychiatrist says."

We needed help, but I felt discarded.

Of course, the wait for an appointment with the psychiatrist was a month and Matt didn't want to attend the scheduled appointment, but I coaxed him into it. In the waiting room, we sat for more than an hour, which offended Matt, "This is just rude. Who makes people wait an hour to see them?"

Finally, the doctor—his hair pulled back in a skinny, limp ponytail—called us in. We answered some questions.

"Do you smoke pot?"

Matt looked at me.

"I don't," I said. I motioned to Matt, smiling and nodding, trying to indicate that he should answer accurately even if he thought his answers would startle or dismay me. Though I didn't often admit it, I knew he smoked weed.

"Do you drink alcohol?"

Doctor Poor-excuse-for-a-pony-tail (not his real name) sorted through the paperwork we'd filled out. Had he read the words on the pages?

If you're going to have a ponytail, have a substantial one, I thought. I imagined pulling out a pair of scissors and discretely snipping his appendage.

"Dr. Windbag referred us to you because Matt was arrested for drunk driving." I reminded. I didn't like to say it. And I didn't like to say it in front of Matt because saying it might increase his shame, but somebody had to steer this conversation. And now I know that I had that learned helplessness thing that my therapist pointed out going on, but even so, I didn't want to wait an hour for an appointment and then dither away the time.

"Do you ever feel like the television is talking directly to you?" the doctor asked Matt.

I felt my face screw into bewilderment. I wanted to have a little tantrum, complete with screaming and foot stamping. I wanted to call out, "Does anyone understand that our family has a problem and we need help, but the television is not part of it."

Maybe the doctor detected my attitude. Maybe it was just time for Matt to be questioned alone. Doctor Poor-excuse asked me to leave the room. I sat in the waiting room, held a magazine wide open, and discretely studied the other occupants. I wondered why they were there. I imagined mentioning, "Your wait might not be worth it." But I was too tired for conversation.

When Doctor Poor-excuse invited me back in, he asked Matt for permission to give me the white slip of paper with a prescription for antidepressants on it. I took the paper, paid the bill and we headed out.

"Did you like his ponytail?" I asked.

"No," Matt stated glumly.

I told Matt how I'd imagined snipping it off. He didn't smile, but almost.

Matt took the prescribed pills for a few days, but said they made him feel funny and he stopped taking them.

Like they say, hindsight is 20/20, but what if I'd demanded right then and there to be equipped. To learn exactly what depression is and how to combat it?

And I'd like to pause my story for a moment and say to you, dear reader, if your loved one is diagnosed with a mental illness, get equipped! Get all the information you can. You might have to hunt for information, but it is available. Being informed will help you chose care that can lead to health and life for you and your loved one.

Chapter fourteen: Life after a DUI

For the offender, the person who has violated civic duty, in this case, my child, life after a DUI arrest includes a lot of waiting for consequences—bracing for the sledgehammer of justice to fall. The wait is not calm or still. It's an intense, clenched, bracing-for-pain, while being exceedingly careful not to show any physical signs of anxiety. Like when you sit in the dentist chair, waiting for the dentist to drill, hear the whine of the drill and steel yourself for pain in case the Novocain hasn't sufficiently numbed you.

For the mother of the offender, in this case, me, life after a DUI arrest includes dread, and some relief. I felt that I could relinquish my groping for control to an experienced, just authority who was going to step in and deal with this problem that I couldn't sort out.

A staunch law-abider, I'd always believed that laws are reasonable and good, and I embraced my civic duty to live by them. However, in the state of Pennsylvania, where we live, the DUI offender's license is not immediately revoked. That bewildered me. Shouldn't a person who's endangered themselves and others by driving drunk be immediately prohibited from driving? For a few months, yes months, after the arrest, Matt still had his license. He still owned a car, and legally, he could still drive. Negotiating this circumstance felt really tricky because he lived at home. Could we accurately and safely conclude that the arrest would deter him from driving drunk again? Or should we seize his keys? What was our responsibility? Step in? Or cede the outcome to existing laws?

Should we try to help Matt hire legal counsel to negotiate his way through the charges? Matt and Steve visited a lawyer who explained—to our relief, because Matt didn't have the money to hire one, and we didn't either—that with a first DUI, a defendant who intended to plead guilty didn't need an advocate. Lawyer or no lawyer, the standard sentence included a substantial fine, mandatory education, eight counseling sessions with a drug and alcohol counselor, and the loss of a driver's license for three months (one year for Matt because, at the time, he was underage).

Eventually, Matt received a big, fat letter by registered mail. It was delivered by our mail carrier who pulled her jeep into our driveway and blasted her horn. She does this whenever she delivers a package that won't fit in our mailbox. I think she should act like the FedEx man who jumps out of his truck and jogs to the porch to deposit a package. It's her job to deliver the mail—not mine to retrieve it. So when I hear her honk, I discreetly extend the time it takes to slip on some shoes, pull on a coat and walk out to her vehicle. Although, some might label my intentional holdup as passive aggressive behavior, I think she deserves to wait.

The day the letter came, after I sauntered to her jeep window, she didn't hand me a package; she thrust a letter and a pen at me: "This has to be signed for." The letter was addressed to Matt and the return address jumped off the corner of the envelope and branded my forehead with shame. I signed as quickly as I could and scurried to the shelter of my house. I don't want to be known as the mother of someone who gets letters from the county prosecutor's office and I'm certain that forever after, the mail carrier will think of me as the mother of the son with criminal charges. In my thoughts, I bargained with her. I promised to stop judging her job performance, if she stops judging me.

The letter listed Matt's charges and included instructions and dates for court appearances. I marked the date on the calendar. But I didn't scribble the words "court date." I jotted "Bellefonte." The courthouse location was all the reminder I could endure.

Without telling Matt, I asked our family doctor, who has cared for Matt regularly over the years, to write a letter detailing Matt's difficulties that we could present to the judge in hopes of prompting a sentence that included extra drug and alcohol counseling. We didn't intend to request less intervention; we wanted more. The doctor's letter was delivered to our house in a sealed envelope and stamped confidential. According to law, anything the doctor and Matt had discussed was private. I placed the letter in my purse to deliver to the judge at the hearing.

On court day, we approached the imposing, stone courthouse that sits high on a hill and due to its architecture and position radiates power. To my dismay, more than once, trailing one of my sons, I've climbed the courthouse steps, walked through the space between the pillars, pushed back the heavy front door, deposited keys and coins in a basket, and inched through a metal detector. The uniformed guard who supervises entries wears a big revolver in a holster on his hip. That gun, snug on his hip, is, for me, like a stubbed toe or aching tooth, the focus of my attention. But the guard acts like the gun isn't there. I guess I think that someone packing a weapon should constantly shout alerts: "Stand back everyone: this is a gun!" However, the guard performs his task like clearing people for entry is as everyday as pulling clothes from a dryer and folding them. For him, I guess, it is. I felt frightened and cowed as I passed him. I wanted to murmur an excuse for my appearance there, but I didn't know one.

The courtroom held a few long benches that look like church pews. The benches were peopled with defendants, and their supporters, like us, in street clothes. Men and women in business suits were scattered through the room: lawyers, I concluded. Police escorted a couple of shuffling men who wore orange jumps suits and metal restraints like handcuffs and some kind of shackles. I scanned the crowd for their mothers and wondered how the women cope.

At the front of the room, a large desk sat on a platform and the judge, dressed in a black robe, sat up higher than the rest of us and brandished a gavel. Instructed by the judge, the court attendant started the hearing. No one explained to us what would happen. I didn't like not knowing. The events happened in rapid succession. As a group, the defendants stood. A court official held a bible. In unison, the defendants promised to tell the truth. As a group, they pleaded guilty to driving under the influence. There was no opportunity to express an individual need, or to say, "I plead guilty, but please consider this extenuating circumstance when you determine my sentence." But there was no spotlight to shrink from, either. No one paid particular attention to my son's trespass.

Matt's name was called, and he walked to the front to sign some papers. He turned in his license. We headed out, relieved to have this occasion behind us.

On the way home, we didn't think of stopping for pizza or ice cream—like we do on some family outings. We both needed a nap. At home, I realized the doctor's letter addressed to the judge was still in my purse. I pulled it out, and hesitated, held by the word stamped on the envelope: confidential. Should I respect that label? I ripped the envelope open and read the letter.

In the message, the doctor described extenuating circumstances that have affected Matt's behavior and—this was news to me—revealed that Matt had been diagnosed with Post-Traumatic Stress Disorder (PTSD).

In our case, the privacy laws that protect an adult's medical information prevented us from learning the severity of our son's medical condition.

After reading the letter, I forgot to nap. I googled PTSD and read the symptoms. I recognized each one: Inability to keep a job, alcohol and drug abuse, erratic behavior, bursts of anger, sleeplessness.

I felt more confused, more inadequate and more fearful. Why had the doctor who'd diagnosed Matt not insisted he get help? Why hadn't the doctor informed us and helped us get help? Did help exist? What had happened to traumatize Matt? Dark imaginings plagued me. Was he brutally hazed? Was he raped? Could men be raped? He's a big guy. I doubted it.

I decided to pry. In those days, Matt had really shut down. If I asked how he felt, I might be met with cold silence or a bristling brush off. He didn't talk much, and I wasn't always sure if my questions made sense to him. In those days, Matt was physically present, but absent in thought, and human connection. His physical body took up space, but the inner spark that makes a person had shriveled and hidden. The part of him that felt and shared ideas and feelings seemed unreachable.

I explained the circumstances of the letter. I said I'd asked the doctor for a letter to give to the judge and the doctor had written a confidential message, but when we weren't able to get it to the judge, I'd read the message. I told Matt what the message said. I asked him what had traumatized him. I thought I had the timing figured out. I knew the when. The event must have happened the night before he showed up drunk at the high school.

"Just tell me what kind of help to look for and we'll find it." I promised that we wouldn't go back to Dr. Windbag or Dr. Poor-excuse. "Just please, tell me what kind of help you need."

He shrugged and said nothing.

Around this time, the writing of Victor Frankl, a psychiatrist who'd survived civic upheaval, authority gone haywire, and the grave injustice of imprisonment in WWII Nazi prison camps, became meaningful to me. Frankl had observed the effect of devastating trauma on his co-prisoners. Some people closed in on themselves. They talked less and less. Their words got trapped inside. Although, Matt had not faced evil and atrocities like Frankl had observed, like those victims, he'd become almost mute. He didn't even try to squirm to set his words free. I fretted because I didn't know how to help him express his thoughts.

Without a license, we hoped Matt would choose independence and start to bike places and get healthy, but that did not happen. Sometimes, I wondered if I should refuse to drive him places. You don't have a license so stay put. But deep down, I felt that if I didn't drive him places, he'd just curl up in bed and sink deeper into depression—if that were even possible. Plus, he needed to get to work to earn money to pay off his fine. I became his chief chauffeur.

I didn't mind driving him. Knowing he wasn't driving drunk—ever—brought me relief. And I thought that when we sat side by side in the car, he had opportunity to talk. If he started to talk, I'd be there to listen. If he indicated what kind of help he needed, I'd be there to know.

Chapter fifteen: Tough Love

Like the individuals Frankl observed, Matt was silent. I was silent, too. I sealed my hurt and thoughts inside for a number of reasons. I was dazed—life was turning out so differently than I had expected, and I didn't know how to react or what to say. I feared that if I let my restraint relax for a moment, strong emotions would overwhelm me and leave me squirming and helpless in the aftermath. I was ashamed of our circumstances, so I didn't talk about them readily. I didn't want to broadcast them. My friends often shared good news of their kids' graduations, weddings, and initial career jobs. I compared our situations in my mind and I didn't want to be the person who spoke of great sadness in every gathering.

So instead of sharing my thoughts and feelings, I loomed silent and listened to other people express their joy as they watched their teens move towards responsible adulthood. I didn't want less forward movement and joy for them, but I wanted some progress for my son. He didn't even need to move towards adulthood at the same speed, but I wanted him to move toward rather than away from healthy, responsible adulthood.

One morning, during those dark years, Matt arrived home after spending the night at a friend's after a party. Someone had dropped him off in our driveway. Thick, black permanent marker lines were scrawled on his face and his chest. At the party, he'd passed out, from alcohol, or maybe drugs, and his friends had written on him.

My treasure's friends had vandalized him, but he laid down and let it happen. I felt so powerless and sad. I gaped. "Just stop," I wanted to insist. But my words, my wishes, didn't carry impact. So, I was mute.

Steve reacted differently. He was angry. He slammed his fist on the table. He yelled loudly that if Matt didn't pull himself up by the bootstraps, get a job, and stop partying, he was going to be kicked out of the house.

I wanted Matt to change, too. I wanted Matt to start living differently. But every cell of me felt that kicking him out of our home was not the answer. Especially during winter in Pennsylvania. If we kicked Matt out, where would he go? He'd burned bridges with many good friends. I didn't want him living with scoundrels who scribbled on him for entertainment when he was down and helpless. He was down and seemed helpless most the time. Thoughtless treatment by drunk, giddy bystanders would destroy him.

Steve's friends observed, accurately, and Steve reported to me, "So and so says I've put up with far more than a father should have to…It's time for Matt to go."

We'd put up with a lot, but I couldn't agree with forcing Matt to leave. When I prayed, and listened for God's response, I heard mostly silence.

One Saturday morning, Matt hobbled home from a night out and plunked down on the couch. One ankle was so swollen, I was sure it was broken. He and his partying companions had gone hiking—while drunk or high—on a treacherous path through the woods and he fell.

On the couch, he grimaced and moaned. He propped his swollen ankle on a pillow and asked me to bring him an ice pack.

As I filled a bag with ice, I thought about Matt's hike in the dark—so foolish. He deserved to feel pain.

Matt's health insurance covered next to nothing. I resented the extra expense medical attention for his injury would cost us. I stomped from the freezer to the couch and dropped the icepack on his lap. I grouched about the inconvenience of rearranging my schedule so that I could take him to the doctor. I wanted Matt to feel the full force of the negative emotions that I felt over the extra work that his predicament was causing me.

In my mind, I staged a little tantrum that only God could hear. "I'm suffering the consequences of his out-of-control partying. It's my schedule—interrupted. It's my money—down the drain."

Steve often said that we needed to show Matt tough love. Matt should experience the consequences of his behavior full force. I think that's what Steve meant by tough love. Let him have what he deserves. He got himself into this. Let him get himself out. That Saturday morning, I was on board with tough love.

Matt called from the couch, "Can somebody get me some toast? I'm hungry."

As the morning progressed and I became more upset, I went to my computer to check email. I planned to email a friend and ask her to pray for me. In my time on the internet, I happened to see a bible verse that described God's love for people. I can't recall exactly the verse but the essence of it is that God loves when people have done nothing to deserve his love. He loves when we've done everything in our power to reject his love. As I read the words, God said to my spirit as clear as if he'd doused me with a pail of ice-cold water: this is your chance to love Matt like I love him. Love whether he deserves love or not. Love whether he responds or not. That's how I'm accustomed to loving. This is your chance to love like I do.

It's not every day we get the opportunity to love like God loves. To love when love is not deserved. To love when it would be easier to withhold love. To love when anger seems reasonable.

Or, maybe, it is every day.

That day, I took the chance. "I want to love him that way, God," I said. My anger dissipated.

I left my chores undone, pulled my purse over my shoulder, grabbed the car keys and said in a reasonable, maybe even compassionate, tone, "Your leg must hurt. Let's go to the clinic."

I know in some circumstances, for some people, tough

love in which a child endures the full consequences of their behavior is reasonable and works.

But, in our case, I learned not to be hasty to jump on the tough love bandwagon. When loving someone who is suffering from a bout of mental illness, the best advice, the information that helped me act most lovingly, came many years into our experience, and was from a nurse who'd worked in the behavioral health unit of a hospital for twenty years. About Matt, she said, "Faith, his brain is broken. That means the part of him that makes good decisions doesn't work right now."

That perspective helped me navigate difficult times. It helped me feel less shame about our circumstances. It helped me find ways to act compassionately. I wouldn't ask a person with a broken leg to walk to work, so why would I ask a person with a broken brain to behave reasonably?

Chapter sixteen: Sharing

So while I could understand Steve's anger, and I often felt angry, too, I could not shake the certain assurance that family means loving unconditionally, and in our case, it meant giving Matt a place to live even though having him around wasn't easy.

Steve fumed and disagreed stridently. Tension built.

One snowy day during winter, Steve stayed home from work because he was not feeling well. Matt was home—unemployed, or at least underemployed—not working forty hours a week. He lounged in his darkened room, either sleeping or playing video games. I went to work worried about the two of them together—an argument was inevitable—but I was glad to be away from the strain.

That afternoon, during the fifteen-minute break between two of my classes, I noticed that I'd missed a call from Steve. As I walked quickly through the drifting snowflakes and biting cold to my next class, I returned the call. Steve picked up and with no pleasantries or small talk, he said abruptly, "I just want to you know, I kicked Matt out. He's packing his backpack and leaving now."

Steve explained his perspective. I'd heard it before. He described the specific events of that day and said that he could no longer tolerate Matt's attitude, video games, and unwillingness to look for work or pull his weight or just do something.

My stomach sank.

"Where will he go?" I asked.

"That's for him to figure out."

I hung up and finished the walk to my class. Turmoil churned and grated in my thoughts. Is there a local homeless shelter? Will Matt know how to find it? He was not functioning as the alert, smart kid I'd once known. He was drowning in life. We had latched him to the lifeboat, kept him afloat for a while, but now the ties were severed. He'd have to swim or sink. I was certain that he would sink. He wasn't capable of surviving on his own.

I walked into the classroom where my class was scheduled to meet. I brushed the snow from my coat and hung it over a chair's back. I carefully placed my mittens on the windowsill above the heater to dry. I pulled my books from my bag and arranged them on the desk in the front of the room. I waited until starting time and in front of twenty-four freshmen students, opened my mouth to start talking. No words came out. Instead, tears streamed down my face. "Excuse me a minute," I squeaked. I left the room and crossed the hall to the restroom. I leaned on the sink, with my head in my hands, and considered cancelling class. But I didn't have anything else to do. At least teaching a class would fill up some of my time and give me something worthwhile to think about.

I blotted my blotched face with cool, wet paper towels. I blew my nose. The mirror revealed that the day's look wasn't my best. I didn't even care. I returned to the classroom and stood quietly for a moment at the front of the room. "Sorry about that. I'm okay now and in the next fifty minutes, we're going to act like learning to write is more important than other things that are going on in my life right now." I felt relieved to say words.

There was a silence, but it was a warm, friendly silence. Then a kid, in the front row—I wish I could remember his name—spoke out. "You have to tell us what's going on."

Did I?

A few of the other students chimed in with murmurs of assent. "Tell us."

Briefly I told them.

Then three or four or maybe five of them said, "He'll be

okay. He'll be back." They shared stories of times they had been kicked out by fathers, stepfathers or mothers and lived on their own for a week, or two, and then—each one—had found their way back home.

Their comments made me think that if Matt could just survive awhile, perhaps Steve would relent and Matt could come back home. In class, we didn't cover much else that day, but the writing that students produced during the rest of the semester was more authentic than the norm. I gained unprecedented insight into student lives. I learned of students' struggles with anxiety, depression, and drugs. One young man wrote about the cocaine addiction he'd developed since coming to college and how worried he was that his parents would find out. I offered to help him find help. He declined my offer and soon dropped the class. Oh, my breaking heart.

Those students were my support section as the semester progressed. They were always eager to start class with an update on my family.

The day of Steve's phone call, after classes were over, I stayed in my on-campus office for a long time. I pushed papers around my desk and thought about grading or commenting on student work. I didn't get hungry. I didn't want supper. Eventually, I decided to go home because Phillip and Carolyn would be there, and I needed a place to sleep.

It was well-past dark and dinner time when I pulled into the driveway. I sat in the car and gazed at the front of the house. Light brightened a window or two. The television flickered through the living room window. Once, the house had been such a happy place. Now it was a place marred by conflict. Knowing what to do when it's time for a kid to grow and they just don't budge is difficult. Matt's unhealthy situation was a little like decay. But it was my decay. I was going to miss that kid. For me, the situation was like having an aching tooth pulled. I would notice his absence every minute of every day.

Would he get in touch with me?

What are the guidelines for navigating the circumstance

of a kicked-out kid?

Could I get in touch with him?

Steve would surely interpret that action as me taking Matt's side in this conflict.

Slowly, I hefted myself out of the car and pulled my book bag over my shoulder. I dragged myself up the steps and into the house. Steve laid on the couch watching television. He greeted me. His voice was flat and without emotion. "Matt's in his bedroom sleeping."

"What?"

"While he was packing, he must have laid down and fallen asleep. I fell asleep, too."

"So is he kicked out?"

"I dunno."

Matt woke up later and made himself a sandwich. He didn't unpack. But he didn't finish packing.

My relief was overshadowed by anger. Why had Steve called me at work, during classes with this alarm that wasn't even an alarm?

I worried that I would lose my husband and my son.

However, the stories I had heard from my students helped me begin to believe there could be a positive outcome for our story. The kids' positive reaction encouraged me to communicate more openly about the turmoil in my life. Through sharing I learned that I wasn't the only one struggling, so I felt less lonely.

Once, as I stood in line at Sherwin and Williams, waiting to buy a gallon of paint, a young man who was also waiting started a conversation. As we talked, the topic of Steve and Matt's relationship came up. I don't recall how we broached the subject...maybe I got a phone call from Steve while I stood in line in which Steve complained about Matt's behavior. Or maybe, to pass the wait, the young man beside me asked, "How are you?"

Often, in passing, someone would voice the polite greeting phrase and I felt forced to the crux of a dilemma. Should I glibly lie, "Fine." Or should I tell the truth? "I am miserable. I am so worried about my son."

That day in line at the paint store while I waited for my

paint to be shaken, I shared openly with the young man who had greeted me. I told him about the father-son conflict in our family.

"I can relate to that," he said. "My Dad and I used to fight all the time. My Dad didn't like my friends. He didn't like how I drove. He didn't think I took good care of my car. He didn't think I worked hard enough."

He paused remembering. "My Dad yelled and swore at me and I yelled back. We never—you know—hit each other. But almost."

"Really?" I was interested in the outcome of his story.

"Really. But now we are best friends. We are working together on a project this weekend. That's why I'm here getting this." He pointed to the painting supplies he had gathered.

"Best friends?" I knew that could never happen for Steve and Matt, but a truce would be nice. "How old are you? When did your relationship turn for the better?"

"It took a few years. We both changed." He couldn't identify what had prompted the change.

My paint was ready. The cashier called for the next in line.

Paint can and paint sticks in hand, I left the store with more than the paint I'd paid for. I felt hopeful. Maybe things could change for Matt and Steve. Maybe someday in the future, a truce could be achieved.

I had learned about the possibility of future peace by sharing glimpses of my pain—by putting it into words and letting others know. I started to talk of my troubles more often. And I learned that talking is one of the tools to use to gain support and health.

Share your story. It's an effective way to start your quest for help and health.

Chapter seventeen: Alcoholic?

"Do. You. Think. He. Is. An. Alcoholic?" Steve's words bored into me. He wanted to pin me down. To force me to state my opinion. I feared there was no correct answer to that question. To me, a "Yes" meant I resigned my son to a life of out-of-control despair. A "No" pushed me into a wide chasm of swirling uncertainties in which I wondered: if not alcoholism, what is his problem?

I didn't think I knew any alcoholics or much about alcoholism. When I considered hopes for my children and their futures, alcoholism sure wasn't included. The only individuals that I had ever come in contact with that I suspected were alcoholics were the Ojibway Indians (As we called them when I was a child; now they are called Native Canadians) who loitered on the street corners of the small downtown where I grew up. When I walked past them, I smelled booze. They usually kept to themselves unless they asked for change so they could buy hairspray and cheese curls. When they couldn't afford drink, they sprayed hairspray on the cheese curls and ate them to get a buzz. Once, I saw a Native Canadian man get upset because he'd accidently purchased hairspray without alcohol in it. Once a drunken man followed me down a block, saying, "Kiss me. Kiss me." They were the alcoholics I'd known and my son was not that.

One day, feeling brave, I googled the definition of alcoholism. I compared the description to the characteristics and behavior I observed in Matt. Someone who drinks a lot.

Check. Someone who drinks every day. I didn't know, but I thought, probably, yes. Someone who finds that drinking interferes with their ability to live a productive life. Something was interfering with Matt's ability to thrive. Someone who drinks in secret. I thought about the empties I'd found hidden behind the couch, in the basement, behind the freezer. He seemed to fit the description. Did that mean he could never stop drinking? That he'd end up on a street corner, begging for change so he could satiate his need for alcohol?

I worried. But I resisted labeling him an alcoholic. What good would that do?

I knew for sure he was a problem drinker. When he drank, he had problems. Big ones.

For someone who is worried about a problem drinker, New Year's Eve is not a welcome holiday. Ever. Alcohol is the focus of so many celebrations. So if someone's out celebrating, alcohol is available—expected, even. People who are not problem drinkers guzzle large amounts of alcohol on New Year's Eve.

For many years, I celebrated New Year's Eves by breathing shallowly and not sleeping. It's as if I think I have a superpower. From a distance, my focused, intense bracing for the worst can prevent my son from being involved in alcohol-fueled mishaps like accidents or fights. So I grit my teeth and brace all night long. The next morning, New Year's Day, during the Rose Bowl Parade as I sip a cup of coffee, I let down my guard. Surely, we'd have heard by then of any alcohol-induced catastrophe involving Matt. We'd made it through another impending disaster.

However, it was a few weeks into January 2010 before I learned of the aftermath of Matt's New Year's Eve drinking to oblivion. I got a message on the home landline answering machine. For years after, when I'd notice the blinking light indicating messages on the machine, I'd feel a tick of terror and flinch. This particular message was for Matt from the State College police saying that Matt should return the call, so they could talk about charges.

"Charges?" I asked when I mentioned the message to Matt.

"Yeah, I got into a bit of trouble on New Year's Eve. The police took me to the hospital. I didn't want to go." He used a lot more words than usual trying to brush off the severity of the event.

"Why did they take you to the hospital?"

That question was answered a few days later when the legal paperwork—another registered letter, delivered by our energetic (like I promised: I'm finished judging her job performance) mail lady—came in the mail. Matt had gotten wasted on New Year's Eve. He ended up unconscious in the hallway of an apartment building. Police picked him up and sent him by ambulance to the emergency room. When he came-to there, knowing that he did not have adequate medical insurance, and worried about how he'd pay, he violently resisted treatment. Police charged him with a few things; the gravest: public drunkenness and disorderly conduct. The charges were classified as misdemeanors and sounded very serious. I googled them. In Pennsylvania, an individual found guilty on such charges might serve up to ninety days in jail.

That possibility coated my thoughts and emotions grim. I felt low. So low. And so helpless. But maybe, at the hearing, if we asked the judge, he would point us to help for Matt. I hoped!

The day of the hearing was an unseasonably warm day in February. I canceled class to attend. Despite all I have learned about the benefits of sharing, I did not share with the students (this was a different group of students) the reason for the cancelation. I was back to being silenced by fear and shame. My sister offered to come to the hearing for emotional support. Steve called from work. He planned to meet us there.

"I thought you were picking Matt up."

"He'll meet us there."

I had reservations about trusting Matt to get there. What if he didn't show and ended up in more legal trouble? What if he drank before court and came in reeking of alcohol?

With the dread that looped over my shoulders far heavier than the book bag that I carried, I walked from my office on campus to the downtown courtroom. I thought about prayers I had prayed with friends that God would intervene and amaze us in this difficulty. I also prayed that God would do whatever it took for this to be the last excessive drinking incident for Matt and that I would be able to thank God for his intervention.

I found the right street, but had trouble finding the building. It didn't dominate a hill like the Bellefonte courthouse. Steve called.

"Are you on your way? We're all here."

"Matt, too?"

"Matt, too."

Matt looked good. He had gotten a haircut and dressed in a long sleeve button down shirt and a pair of khakis.

There was no guard and no metal detector to walk through. I guess it was a different kind of court. A receptionist greeted Matt in the foyer and said, "I'll tell the judge you've arrived. He likes to start on time." The hearing was scheduled for two thirty.

Matt was the only defendant.

Matt, Steve, my sister and I entered the courtroom and sat down on the pew-like benches. The clock read two twenty-five. I looked for Matt's lawyer. Two weeks earlier, Matt had reported meeting with a public defender who was slated to guide him through the hearing. The lawyer hadn't arrived yet.

I felt nervous. What happened to defendants found guilty? Would they handcuff Matt in front of us and drag him off to jail? I didn't know. If Matt got jail time, I didn't think he'd survive. He seemed fragile to me. I didn't think he could stand up for himself if someone picked on him. I'd heard they do that in jail. Pick on the new people. I chewed on my bottom lip.

"Where's Matt's lawyer?" Steve asked.

"I don't know. Matt, you met with a lawyer, right?"

"Yes. He said he'd be here." Matt spoke tersely.

When the clock hands indicated two thirty exactly, the black robed judge swept into the courtroom and sat down at the large desk in the front. He perused the papers in front of him and then looked at Matt, "Mr. McDonald, I see your lawyer's not here yet. Would you like to wait? Or reschedule?"

I didn't know rescheduling was an option. Matt should wait for the lawyer.

"No, Sir. I'd like to get this over with."

All three of us—Steve, my sister and I—gasped a little. Shouldn't Matt wait?

"Let's get started then."

"Yes, Your Honor." I felt proud that Matt spoke politely. He might have an outrageous drinking problem, but at least when he was sober, he remembered his manners.

The judge looked at the clock on the wall that now read two thirty-five. "I like to start proceedings on time. The policeman who wrote up these charges," he waved the papers, "telephoned to tell me that he's going to be twenty minutes late."

There was time for the lawyer to arrive. I felt relieved. Matt should call him and tell him to hurry. I leaned to whisper to Matt, "Call your lawyer."

The judge boomed on. "So there's no one here to bring any charges against you. That means that you're not guilty. Come up here and sign these papers."

For a moment, Matt was so startled he didn't move. The judge said again. "With no one here to charge you, you're not guilty, you're not going to jail, and these charges will not be on your record. Get up here and sign these papers."

Matt moved to the front of the room and signed where the judge told him to sign. The judge picked up the papers, said curtly, "Thank you, Mr. McDonald," and left the room.

My thoughts were spinning. I'd spent weeks convincing myself that my son could live through jail and that I could survive a jail term...and what had the judge said?

As we collected our thoughts and pulled our coats on, the policeman who'd written the charges burst into the courtroom. "I'm here."

"The hearing is over. The judge has already left the room," the court assistant informed him.

I guess the policeman felt gypped. He thrust his angry

face in Matt's face and spoke stridently about the serious nature of the charges and the detrimental effects of drinking oneself into a stupor. Everything he said was accurate. But I didn't appreciate his belligerent manner.

"Come on, Matt. You don't have to listen to him."

"I wasn't on time because I was on a drug bust." He fumed.

We didn't get the help we needed, but I was glad that Matt had escaped jail time. I replayed the words in my head. No accuser. No charges. Not guilty. It seemed like extravagant grace. At least, on that day.

I've told a lot of people this story and their reactions are interesting. None would have given that much grace. Some get a little panicked, "But does your son understand? Does he realize?"

Matt understood that he'd narrowly escaped an uncomfortable stint and that he had drinking problems. I found a folded note that he had written and intended to give to the judge. It said:

> I would like to apologize to the court and the arresting officers for wasting your time. And I would like to apologize for my actions and tell you that I have learned from my mistake. I won't let alcohol abuse be a part of my life anymore because all it causes is problems for me and my family. Also, I feel that the fines for my crimes would be a sufficient punishment enough for me and that I don't need jail time to learn that I need to stop abusing alcohol. I am currently seeking counseling from a pastor at a local church for alcohol abuse among other things.

For a long time, every day, no matter what we were doing—washing dishes, folding laundry, skiing, I had to resist saying to Matt, "Well, this sure beats visiting you in jail."

Would relief and resolve be enough to help Matt put

excessive drinking behind him and move forward in a positive direction?

Chapter eighteen: It's a family thing

We muddled through days which turned into months which turned into years. The events blur and some points of pain stick out in my memory more than others. Matt would take a baby step forward and three giant steps back. The backward steps whisked us to circumstance and emotions that seemed overwhelming, and our bearings were skewed like when Matt fled because he feared that Steve and I were going to murder him (mentioned in chapter one). I know that people take backward steps in life, but sometimes, the steps Matt took back seemed like they'd been lifted from another family's script.

Once as I pushed my cart in a grocery store, I noticed a family shopping all together. The dad moved slowly through the aisle in a motorized cart. The mother walked haltingly behind pushing a grocery cart which held a pile of groceries and a cute kid who looked about three- years-old. The kid reached and grabbed a box of crackers off a shelf.

The woman snatched the box from the child and scolded. "Just stop that. Mommy won't love you if you do that again."

Her statement made me angry. Who uses love as a bargaining chip in discipline?

She called to the man who motored ahead. "Benny isn't behaving. I told him that if he didn't stop, we wouldn't love him anymore."

"Stop that or Mommy and Daddy won't love you," the man growled and glared at the child.

I thought that I would collapse on the floor weeping. I

could imagine all the disaster we had encountered happening to that family. It would make sense if that family's children couldn't do life because they feared that love would be snatched from them because of a grocery store mishap. But my son? Why couldn't my son thrive? I learned the answer, years later—he was overwhelmed with mental illness.

Once a friend said to me, "Your kids know that you'll love them no matter what. It gives them the freedom to misbehave."

Of course, I was going to love my kids no matter what. Isn't unconditional love a tenet of effective parenting? I felt violence in my heart against those love-snatching grocery store parents. I wanted to scold them vehemently. But I didn't.

I cried inside. I was perplexed as to why our family's love wasn't enough to get Matt's life righted.

But maybe, with time, it would be. In the fall of 2010, Matt had returned to college in Williamsport—his third attempt at college. He selected a new major—forestry—and within weeks it looked like he might be on his way out of the extended slump. He still partied some weekends. But more often, he studied. One Saturday, he left home for a party and came back a few minutes later, saying he'd decided staying in and studying was a better choice. He wasn't gregarious, by any means. He was still sullen and stingy with words. But he did work hard to succeed in classes.

That same fall, fourteen-year-old Carolyn tried to convince me that I should accompany her on a trip to Haiti for ten days before Christmas. Matt's well-being was still very much a concentrated focus of my heart. Despite my learned helplessness, I seemed to think that my presence and my worry were necessary for his forward movement. Also, I often intervened when he and Steve argued. However, I determined to pry myself from my post and go with Carolyn.

I was gone for ten days and when I got home, my family was still intact. In fact, while we were away, it had grown. Steve had purchased a Golden Retriever puppy. We knew our older dog Colby (a thirteen-year-old Golden Retriever) was fading and would die soon and we knew that the kids—especially Matt— (and Steve) would grieve ferociously. We thought that the presence of a new puppy might make losing the old dog easier.

Our attempt to distract them from their pain angered Carolyn. She felt it diminished the contribution that Colby had made to the family. He'd been our well-loved pet for a lot of years.

Matt loved Colby and he liked the new dog. For a couple of weeks, the old dog seemed enlivened by the puppy. Then the old dog took a drastic turn. He started spitting up blood. We knew it was time to take him to the vet, so she could put him down. But we wanted the kids to have a chance to say good-bye. So we called Matt and Phillip who were away at school and offered them the opportunity to come home and say good-bye. They both came. Matt said that he'd stay home and spend the night with Colby. Matt made Colby a sleeping bag bed in the garage and slept on the floor beside him, rousing to pet the dog when he seemed uncomfortable. In the morning, Steve, Matt and Carolyn took the dog, who could barely walk and whose breathing was labored, to the vet to be put to sleep. That afternoon, we held a short funeral service in our backyard. Carolyn wailed and raged. She piled all Colby's toys and his dog bed together and took them to her room. That puppy, the cute puppy who was still alive would not inherit or enjoy the benefits of any of Colby's stuff. She snapped at the puppy whenever he came near her.

Matt didn't cry at all. He stoically packed his backpack, scratched the puppy's head and headed back to school. It was one, maybe two weeks later, that he called home and declared, "I'm quitting school. I can't do it. People don't like me here."

We tried to talk him into taking a week off, into meeting with a counselor before making the decision to quit. He was adamant. "I can't do it. I need to come home."

Things were dismal for Matt at home. He didn't have a job. Or anything to do. He rattled around in the house aimlessly. Sometimes, he'd lay on the couch, watching television and I'd peek into the room and see tears streaming from his eyes. I thought maybe the tears were a good sign. Maybe they expressed emotion too long squelched. I didn't know for sure.

"What bothers you most?" a friend asked me.

"What bothers me most? Everything!" I said.

"But what bothers you most?" She persisted and pressed me to identify one thing.

I concluded that the waste bothered me most. Our precious son's life was wasting away in front of us and we did not know how to stop the squandering.

I prayed and prayed. I wrote my prayers on an index card that I carried with me. Every time I worried about Matt, I pulled the index card out and prayed for him.

One morning after my drive to work as I emerged from my car in the parking lot, the sun rising over Mount Nittany stopped me. As I noticed the beauty, a strong message from God invaded me. "None of this is wasted. I will not waste a moment of this experience."

My whole self was filled with a knowing that Matt's experience would not be wasted. Knowing that helped to ease the pain a little.

Chapter nineteen: Refused…

Steve, an extrovert, knowing how lonely Matt was, occasionally talked him into going downtown to walk around with the new puppy, who we'd named Ollie, on a leash.

"It's a good way to meet people. Everyone stops to pet Ollie."

One Saturday evening, after they had walked around downtown with the puppy and interacted with a number of puppy admirers, Steve came home with the puppy and Matt went for a drive. At that time, he had a license. I waited awake for a long time listening for him come in. He didn't. Early in the morning the phone rang. It was Matt. He'd been driving intoxicated and crashed his car into a stump in an elderly lady's yard. After crashing, he had gotten out of the car, and walked into her garage. She heard him, came to investigate, and invited him to come in and sleep on her sofa. The next morning, her son came and lectured Matt on the dangers of driving drunk, helped him get his car unstuck and told him to call home.

This incident was the second time Matt's drunken trespass had been met with kindness. I wondered how many chances he would get.

Matt paid for his car's repairs and promised repeatedly to never drive drunk again. "I have learned my lesson," he said.

I reiterated the dangers and consequences of drunk driving. I did not find any comfort in his promises to never drive drunk. I didn't think I could believe them. However, he'd spent all his money on car repairs, and he didn't have a job. I calmed my worries by telling myself that he couldn't buy alcohol because he had no money.

Finally, I talked him into seeing a doctor who prescribed an antidepressant for him. Maybe the omission didn't make a difference, but no one, not the doctor, not the pharmacist, described to Matt the dangers of drinking while taking antidepressants. He was on the medication for three days. The third day was a Saturday. To get him out of bed, Steve offered to pay him to clean and detail our truck. Matt did a great job on the truck. I wasn't home when Steve paid him in cash. When I arrived home, and saw Matt wasn't there, I said in a panic to Steve, "Where's Matt?"

I knew that Matt with money couldn't be a good thing.

"Do you think I should go look for him?"

"Where would you look?"

We waited up a long time. Eventually, I crawled into bed beside Steve and dozed fitfully until the phone rang. Steve answered it because it is his job to answer the telephone when it rings in the night.

Driving on a winding road, Matt had rolled his car. He'd climbed out the shattered window, seemingly unhurt, but had been arrested for drunk driving and was at the county jail. Could we pick him up?

Under the covers, Steve and I held hands in a rare moment of solidarity. We could face this challenge. Together.

When we picked Matt up at the jail, he was agitated and belligerent. He yelled at us. "I'm not staying with you. I'm packing up my stuff and leaving. I don't belong here with you. I'm not your son."

We tried to soothe him. "You are our son. We love you. We can get through this."

He shouted and swore. "I'm leaving. I'm getting my backpack and just leaving."

We talked him into sleeping first. "You're tired. Get some sleep. You can leave in the morning, if you still feel like leaving."

In the morning, Steve went to church. I stayed home and waited for Matt to wake up. I called a good friend. I whimpered, "Matt totaled his car last night driving drunk. And when we picked him up, he was talking nonsense. I don't know what to do."

"Where is he now?"

"Sleeping."

"He's safe?"

"Yes."

"All you have to do is breathe. Breathe in. Breathe out. Can you do that?"

"Yes." I squeaked and I sat on the couch. I breathed in. I breathed out. That practice would get me through many hard times.

When Matt woke up, he was still talking nonsense. With the aid of a crisis counselor, we convinced him to go to a mental health facility. The decision to talk him into going was hard for me because I held two misconceptions that I now find so silly. One: people land in mental health facilities because they've failed morally. They've done something really wrong to get there. Two: mentally ill people do not get better. I thought once mentally ill, mentally ill for a lifetime.

The facility required that Matt sign himself in for a minimum of three days. He did. But as soon as he was admitted, he wanted out. We think a psychiatrist saw him while he was there, but we don't know for sure. Matt said his surroundings were unwelcoming; other patients moaned and made strange sounds and that he couldn't even go to the bathroom without asking permission.

On the morning of the third day, we were invited to attend a meeting. I was so nervous. At the facility, we were buzzed through a couple of locked doors and told to wait in a conference room. The social worker entered, introduced herself and lectured us in a patronizing manner. She said that Matt was leaving too early. That they didn't really know what his problem was. Nothing had been determined or resolved. He hadn't been diagnosed. "Do you understand that?"

Numb, we probably nodded. All I knew is that I didn't like how I was being treated and that I probably didn't like how she'd treated Matt.

She spat words at me, "He refuses to participate in his own recovery." I felt like she wanted to slap me. She seemed to imply that if we were better people our son would participate in his recovery.

I knew that Matt's unwillingness to participate was a facet of our problem. But how was it a problem for an expert in the field? As a longtime teacher of required college classes, I have become skilled at luring students into participating in their own education. Didn't she have ways to coax or encourage people to participate in their recoveries?

Memories of our visit to that facility feel like road rash in my mind. I can't imagine how it must feel for Matt to recall that time in his life.

We had a problem that we couldn't solve. We didn't know if anyone else ever encountered a similar problem. The experts from whom we'd hoped to get help didn't know what to do.

Steve called around and found another facility. This one concentrated on rehab. But the day that Matt was scheduled to go, he panicked, and we couldn't convince him to get in the car. He refused to participate in his own recovery.

Chapter twenty: Letters

The waiting for the court date for the drunk-driving charge was difficult. Matt seemed more diminished than ever before. I hoped that in court we would get some help. Maybe we'd meet an expert who would show us how to lure Matt into recovering.

Eventually, Matt appeared in court where he pled guilty. The hearing was in the Bellefonte, high-on-a-hill, courthouse. I wrote another letter in hopes of giving it to the judge. Although as I reread the letter preparing to include it here, I wonder why I hadn't learned that the legal proceedings don't include the exchange of letters. I never got to give my letter to the judge. You're not surprised, and I guess I wasn't, either.

> Your Honor,
> Our son Matt McDonald who is appearing before you today regarding charges of driving under the influence is a loving, sensitive, smart kid with an infectious grin and an amazing sense of humor, but you won't see that today because depression, anxiety and alcohol have taken a toll on his life in the past five years. He needs help breaking this cycle of unhealthy habits and we respectfully request that you consider the following when you determine his sentence:
> Matthew has been struggling with a cycle

of depression, anxiety and problem drinking for five years.

Finding help has been a difficult, frustrating experience; however, since the April 2 incident, Matt has met a few times with an experienced counselor, and we have seen improvement in Matt's behavior and outlook.

Matthew has struggled since graduating from high school. He's tried college three times and been fired from many jobs. His drinking behavior has caused him many problems.

We have tried repeatedly and desperately to get help for him. Getting help is not easy. Over the past five years, Matt visited five different counselors a handful of times. None were a good match for him. The counselor that Matt has seen a few times since the DUI, has developed some rapport with Matt.

Matt has seen our family doctor numerous times, also. At one time, the doctor diagnosed him with post-traumatic stress disorder and another time with chronic anxiety and depression. The doctor has prescribed medication. During fall semester 2010, Matt took medication and successfully completed his best semester in college so far. Then he stopped taking the medication.

In February 2011, in the midst of a panic attack, Matt withdrew from school at the Pennsylvania College of Technology. He returned home and in the following weeks, we tried to find help. Matt visited the Penn State anxiety clinic, but because the session was videotaped, he felt very uncomfortable and decided not to return. Depression and anxiety gained greater hold on him. The week before the DUI he said he felt worthless and hopeless. Many times that week, we noticed him weeping, but he could not tell us why. He spent a lot of time in bed with his covers over his head, answering most questions with the words, "I don't care." He was emotionally flat.

Please consider these things as you determine Matt's sentence. We understand that Matt's sentence could include jail. We fear that jail would exacerbate his depression and anxiety. We have also heard that house arrest is a possibility. Matt has been working regularly for the past five weeks. If he is granted house arrest, would it be possible for him to continue working?

Also, we believe that house arrest alone would not provide Matt the tools that he needs to overcome depression and anxiety and begin to build a productive life.

Since the DUI, we have strongly encouraged Matt to seek counseling. He has tried three options and has repeatedly seen the counselor who seems to be most helpful to him. We request that the sentence you order for Matt would provide strong incentive for his continued participation in counseling.

Respectfully,
Faith and Steve McDonald

Chapter twenty-one: Ankle bracelet

I rarely acknowledged my stealthy desire to be the standard by which the quality of a loving successful parent was measured.

I grew up as a pastor's daughter and in the church that I was raised in, I was taught that a good Christian family was an example to others of what a family living for Christ was like. I thought I could do that—be an example. I thought that was the goal: our family—a stellar example.

When parenting was easy, well, parenting was never easy, but when my kids were behaving within the range of normal, I thought that people could watch me to see how Christian parenting was done.

When our kids were in school, every year on back-to-school night, along with all the other eager parents, Steve and I, intentionally present, visited their classrooms and folded ourselves to fit on the little chairs. Our family lived in a school district where most parents are involved, and the classrooms were almost always packed with parents who listened to the teacher's welcome and teaching philosophy and wanted to find ways to bolster their son's or daughter's education.

Having that many parents present and supportive is unusual, I think.

And it's a good thing, but the competition makes it more difficult to be outstanding. Like how was I going to be recognized as an example of an excellent mother when the other mothers were creating cookies that looked like school buses or alphabet letters in calligraphy, and volunteering to show up at the school and cut little shapes out of construction paper, or to work in the nurse's office and assist vomiting or bleeding kids?

The cookies I bake, while they taste good, are different sizes of approximate round. I can't bare the tedium of cutting shapes. When I was fifteen, I was a volunteer nurses' aide for five minutes—and although I really liked the uniform (white with red pinstripes)—I realized any liquid oozing out of a body made me so queasy I had to vacate my post in the children's ward and spend the rest of my only shift as a junior medical helper hiding in the bathroom.

I wanted to be an outstanding mother in a don't-rock-the-boat-kind-of-way but I couldn't do cookies or shapes or nurse's office volunteer hours. Once, I was invited to shelve library books. I was thrilled to contribute. I wasn't noticed for my contribution. In fact, in my sphere, nobody needed to watch me because they were doing a pretty good job and many of their kids were excelling.

Each fall when we sat in those little chairs, I realized that being noticed would be up to my kids. The teachers often said, "I don't just call home to report bad things like misbehavior or not keeping up with the work, I call to share and celebrate good things. So, if you get a call from me, don't assume I'm calling with bad news."

I wanted one of those celebratory calls. One for each of my kids. I mean, why not? Our achievements are worth celebrating.

My three kids each spent thirteen years in public school. That's 7,020 days. And not once did I get a call for a positive reason. I used to think that somebody else got those calls. But over the years, I've become cynical. I've concluded that while the teachers liked to make that claim, or maybe their bosses pushed them to announce that practice, teachers didn't follow through with the action. Maybe they intended to call and just never got around to it, for what teacher has time to report on the positive? That report can always be put off for another day. And a teacher's work is never finished.

In the absence of positive calls regarding my kids, at least there weren't too many negative calls. Maybe two for Matt from kindergarten through graduation. I do remember getting a call from a middle school teacher, in the evening, after a field trip. I could just tell from the tone of her voice in the greeting that the call's purpose was not to report good behavior.

I developed a habit of going out of my way to avoid Matt's English teachers when he was in eleventh and twelfth grade. His homework habits included an excessive amount of procrastinating and shoddy last-minute work. If I saw the teacher, I might feel the need to explain why he wasn't the rock star English student I wanted him to be and why he didn't cooperate in his own education. I didn't have an explanation.

I wanted my kids to be the stars and the world to be an applauding audience. Silly, I know now.

I have learned that the world admires a narrow range of behaviors and if an individual's behavior is outside that range then he doesn't gain admiration. Or tolerance. Or kindness. He is judged. Sometimes harshly.

When Matt was ill, and his symptoms were often evident, I wanted people to overlook these behaviors and see a person in need of compassion.

When Matt was most anxious, he looked grumpy or annoyed. In the throes of deep anxiety, he involuntarily engaged in nervous habits that distracted people around him. Two of Matt's most distracting habits were lack of eye contact and a nervous laugh. When Matt was involved in a conversation or interaction (which were few), he'd look away and stare into space. If an individual tried to make eye contact with him, he'd shift his gaze. Using appropriate eye contact is a skill that most of us exercise without thought. When a person does not make appropriate eye contact, we notice and assume they feel negative emotions or possess unhealthy traits. We think that a person who doesn't make eye contact has something to hide. Or a person who shifts their gaze lacks confidence.

Sometimes, Matt, aware of this nervous habit, would strive to make eye contact. His brown eyes wide, he'd stare into a person's eyes until the stare created discomfort for the person, who would then look away.

Matt also developed a nervous chuckle. Sometimes, sitting alone, he'd chuckle. Steve always noticed and commented, "There he goes again." I didn't really notice the chuckle. People can sit alone and sigh and nobody gets alarmed, so why panic over a chuckle?

However, a chuckle or nervous laugh is also easily misinterpreted. Especially if the matter at hand is serious.

And after Matt's second DUI, he faced some serious interactions with people in charge. In Pennsylvania, at that time, the sentence for a second DUI was stiffer than for a first. In addition to classes and counseling sessions with a court-approved counselor, the penalties included a large fine and forty-five days of house arrest. That means the individual wears an electronic bracelet on his ankle. If he leaves his house, the bracelet sends a signal that alerts a probation officer. If the outing is not scheduled, the police are sent to arrest the individual. To be set up for house arrest, the sentenced individual must visit the high-on-a-hill courthouse where the corrections officer sets up the conditions, clamps on the bracelet, and arranges a home visit to install the monitoring machine.

I was out of town when Steve drove Matt to the courthouse to be outfitted, but Steve told me what happened. They climbed the stairs to the third floor and sat on a bench in the hall waiting for the appointment. When the probation officer called Matt in to her office, Steve whispered, "Make eye contact. Be polite. Don't chuckle."

Matt nodded.

During the interview, the probation officer asked Matt how to get to his house. He said, "You go to the park and take a left."

She said, "Talleyrand Park?"

Matt told me later that he had never heard the park called Talleyrand Park before. The name Talleyrand struck him funny and he chuckled.

The probation officer immediately declared that their meeting was not a laughing matter and that Matt should stop acting like he thought it was.

Due to nervousness, he laughed again. And she sent him to the hall to sit on a bench and said his flippant attitude meant house arrest was no longer an option. He was headed to jail.

I was in Connecticut, visiting my parents and can remember the spot on the lawn where I was sitting when Steve called me. I can still feel the damp grass moist through my cotton shorts. Steve was upset. Neither of us believed that Matt had the mental stamina to survive jail. Though we didn't know much of what goes on in jail, the stuff we imagined—sitting in a small room, behind bars, with people who were less than cordial—we thought those circumstances would drive Matt into deeper depression. If deeper depression were possible.

I knew Matt's attitude wasn't flippant. He was afraid. "Can you explain to her that anxiety stirs up Matt's nervous laughter? Can she overlook his behavior? And notice that he needs help?"

"I don't know if she'll even speak to me." Steve said.

In Connecticut, we prayed. I sat on the grass, worrying and waiting for Steve's report and I wondered how many folks get mired in deep legal trouble because, due to mental illness, their actions are noticed and misinterpreted. It was at moments like this that we wondered if we should have helped Matt find a lawyer to help him navigate the maze of legal requirements.

The probation officer refused to talk to Steve. "Matt's an adult," she stated.

After a lengthy wait, she called Matt back into her office. He was able to talk to her without chuckling. Our prayers staved off the nervous laughter.

Later that day, a law enforcement officer visited our home and installed the monitor that functioned by being attached to a landline and reported location of the ankle bracelet. It was programed to allow Matt to go to work washing dishes at a local restaurant five days a week at three-thirty in the afternoon. He had to return home by eleven-thirty in the evening. He was scheduled to attend drug and alcohol classes every Monday evening. As long as he kept to that schedule, Matt could be anywhere in the house or on the porch and the machine would send a satisfactory report.

Our house is not large, so there was not a lot for Matt to do. He completed some home improvement projects that we'd been planning to do for some time. Sometimes, he was so bored, he'd fold all the laundry for fun. We moved a ping pong table into our living room and every night after dinner, we played ping pong for at least an hour. While Matt was home all the time, and physically present, a large part of him was still inaccessible. Sometimes, when we played ping pong, he'd smile. Together, we counted the days, but they weren't horrible days. Just confined days.

One day, I got home from work and the machine's alarm was blaring. Alone all day, Matt had decided he'd needed a cigarette and marched out the front door, taken Steve's truck and driven to a nearby convenience store. The action placed him in legal jeopardy in two ways. One, for violating the terms of the house arrest arrangement, he could be taken directly to jail. Two, his license had been confiscated so he wasn't supposed to be driving at all. What if he'd been caught?

I tensed as I waited for a swat team to descend on our home and cart Matt off to jail. The alarm wailed for a while and then the noise got irritating and, although we'd been told not to, we unplugged the machine. The alarm stopped. We plugged that machine back in.

The swat team did not show. Ever. The world hadn't convened and appointed a task force to respond to our son's jailbreak. To our relief, nobody noticed. We didn't even get a phone call. But I wasn't really relieved. I worried that if Matt got away with violating the conditions of house arrest once, he might violate them again.

Chapter twenty-two: Lockout

Over the next year, stalled, sad and silent, but seemingly stable, Matt met all the requirements of his sentence. He paid his four thousand dollar fine with money from his dishwashing job, survived forty-five days of house arrest, bummed rides through the months of no license, and attended the twenty required classes and eight counseling sessions. He had earned the privilege of a restored license, and I thought that the independence that comes with driving might prompt him forward.

But then we learned of another requirement, another expense for a broke individual. A few weeks before Matt was eligible to get his license back, he received a letter from the Pennsylvania Department of Transportation stating that a newly implemented Pennsylvania law required DUI offenders to have an ignition interlock device installed on their cars. The offender must provide proof of an equipped car or the state retains his license. The device requires drivers to blow into a breathalyzer which detects alcohol. If no alcohol is detected, the car will start. If alcohol is detected, then the car will not start. The offender must pay for the device—its installation and monthly maintenance.

You may recall that Matt had totaled his car on the night of his accident, so he didn't own a vehicle to equip. I thought that equipping a car with a breathalyzer was a good idea and I wished the police had told me such devices existed a few years prior when I had worried about Matt driving drunk. I would have insisted he get one.

Since Matt didn't have a car, I offered to equip my car with the device. The offer was naïve. I didn't know that the procedure for blowing into an ignition interlock device is complicated and requires skill. I thought an individual blew once—a short puff—to start the car. I didn't know that original blow, the one required to start the car, called for three lungfuls of breath expelled in a complicated rhythm and punctuated with a hum. I didn't know that a running retest requirement caused the device to blare at irregular intervals during travel, and that when the alarm sounded, the driver had a short window of time in which to perform the intricate blow. After three blowing errors the car stopped operating and the owner was fined. I didn't know that the installers and maintainers of the device served their customers with a large helping of disdain.

Because I didn't know and maybe even if I had, to help Matt clear this final hurdle, one day in August 2012, we drove my car forty-five miles to the installer's location. I wondered how other unlicensed people got their cars to the installers. Matt was fortunate to have support and I think he knew it. We endured the scorn of the installer, who I'll call Larry—his fulltime job is lumberjack—and sat through how-to operate the ignition interlock device video lessons played on a television in Larry's shag carpeted rec-room. He said we had to finish watching the videos before his wife got home. "She don't like strangers watchin' television in her rec room."

While we watched the videos, Larry equipped the car. Part of the process included dismantling the car door and when he put everything back together there was an extra piece left over.

"Yinz save that and in a year when I take the machine out, I'll put the piece back." He handed it to me.

Then he brought out a practice ignition interlock blowing device and told us to take some time to practice blowing. In most cases, I'm a fast learner. Except, it seems, when attempting to perfect an intricate blowww-hummm to start a car. While I hadn't had an alcoholic drink in half a decade, I couldn't muster the breath and the rhythm to pass the test. Finally, when Larry looked away to shuffle some paperwork,

Matt blew for me.

"I'll coach you at home," Matt whispered.

The installer glared. I think he knew something fishy was going on. "Yinz think you can get that car started?"

Matt blew. I drove.

However, the next day, without Matt's company, I had to drive from Pennsylvania to New Jersey to pick up my daughter and nieces at the airport. I am a cautious driver, accustomed to driving in central Pennsylvania, where traffic is not too heavy and people are not too hurried, but even in those conditions my leisurely driving habits prompt an occasional horn blare from an annoyed driver. As I neared New Jersey, the route became unfamiliar and the traffic stream became filled with hasty and aggressive drivers. At first, I held my own and capably accelerated into lanes, forcing traffic to allow me a space. I knew any hesitation could prompt an angry horn blare or a missed turn. But at erratic intervals when the interlock machine beeped loudly, I got frazzled. The beep startled me every time. If I focused on bracing for it, I couldn't concentrate on keeping up with the traffic stream. I imagined the headline: interstate traffic pile up caused by distracted mother who can't master the ignition interlock blow.

After I picked the girls up, the sun set. Driving in the dark on unfamiliar roads is even more challenging to me than driving in daylight. While the act—a passenger completing the blowing when a device is installed on a car—is illegal, Carolyn, sitting in the front passenger's seat, quickly mastered the technique.

"Don't let any police see you blowing!" I insisted. I imagined the conversation with the officer who stopped us.

Turns out, Carolyn's illegal exhaling into the interlock machine's mouthpiece was not the circumstance that eventually brought the police into our interlock experience.

With the device installed, I knew Matt couldn't drive drunk and that brought me a large amount of relief. Almost enough to balance out the occasional inconvenience caused by the machine's flaws which occasionally interfered with the car's operating. We learned again and again that the ignition interlock system needs some fine-tuning.

On September 5, about three weeks after the device had been installed, Matt got ready to go to work early, and the car wouldn't start. He called Larry who reacted as if Matt was trying to drive while intoxicated. I got on the phone to explain that neither of us had been drinking anything but water and both of us needed to get to work. Soon.

Larry, the technician, explained that he was on his way to South Carolina to see his son who was coming home from an army stint in Afghanistan and was unable to help us. "I can help you on Saturday," he said.

Saturday was three workdays away.

"That's unacceptable," I said.

"Me seeing my son is more important than me fixing that machine."

What? Had he just said apples were oranges?

As the technician responsible for a state mandated device that was installed in my car and keeping it from operating, I believed he should have designated a professional to service his clients while he was out of town. I said so.

He huffed and puffed. I reminded him that my son was actually paying him for a service, but that to continue to pay Matt needed to get to work. Finally, after I pressed him for service, Larry said that maybe his boss Mike would help us out.

After four phone calls, I got through to Mike who told me, "This wouldn't have happened if you hadn't tried to drink and drive. And tell your son not to try to drive after he's been drinking."

I explained—at first, calmly and patiently—that I was sober, and my son was sober.

When Mike said, "I've heard that story before. The bottom-line is don't drink and try to drive," I became a little adamant.

After a lengthy conversation, Mike said he'd have another technician service our car. Calvin called and said he would give me a code; I could enter the code into the machine's computer and start the car. Then, within six hours, I would have to drive to Harrisburg (an hour and a half drive) where he could fix the machine. I guess they forgot I had a job to get to.

"Seriously? I have a state mandated device on my car. I am a client, paying your company a hundred dollars a month for a state-mandated service and I have to drive 150 miles to have it serviced? Who manages your company's contract with the State of Pennsylvania?"

"I'm uncomfortable talking about this," he said.

"Of course, you're uncomfortable. This is your cash cow," I exclaimed.

During our conversation, I'd done the math. All numbers are estimates but say there are 10,000 DUI second offenders in the State of Pennsylvania every year (according to available statistics that's a low estimate). They each have to pay a thousand dollars per year to have an ignition interlock system installed on their car and maintained…that's ten million dollars per year at stake.

I told Calvin about the results of my calculation. "Is that why you're uncomfortable talking about it? I'm just asking. Now, who's your company contact?"

Rather than giving me a contact name, he decided that he would drive to my home to service my car in the morning. That day, Matt and I had to find alternate rides to work.

Our second lockout occurred months later in April 2013 when Matt was hospitalized. Steve had driven the car to work and when he was ready to return home, the interlock machine locked him out and indicated that he had been trying to start the car while intoxicated. Steve called on a nearby policeman to breathalyze him and document that he had not been drinking alcohol. When contacted, Larry, the interlock technician, said, "Someone must have been trying to drive while intoxicated."

When Steve explained that police documentation proved that he wasn't intoxicated, Larry said, "Well, your son, then."

When Steve explained that our son was hospitalized and not driving anywhere, Larry said, "Don't tell anyone that. If they find that out they will extend the length of time he's required to have the interlock system installed."

Really? Who is they and is it possible for them to do this?

Our third lockout occurred on August 16, 2013. The compulsory period for the machine to be latched to our car was almost over. Matt was giving a friend a ride and the machine locked him out of the car. We contacted Larry who for once, didn't even mention the possibility of alcohol. He said, "There must be moisture in the machine causing it to malfunction. Why don't you come get a new component for the machine?"

The machine's benefits could entice me to overlook its flaws. The attitudes of the service people were more difficult for me to endure. Each time we were locked out of the car, it was due to the machine's flaws, yet each time, the technicians approached the situation as if we were breaking the law by trying to drive intoxicated. They wielded their power with scorn. Matt was fortunate because he had Steve and I to staunchly vouch for him and declare that the lockout was not due to alcohol. Even so, we were fined twice. We didn't squawk about the fines because who do you appeal to? And what happens to offenders who do not have anyone to vouch for them?

The aspect of having the ignition interlock attached to my car that I hated most was the humiliation. In a parking lot, I glanced around furtively before I huffed and puffed to start my car. Would anyone notice me and wonder what I was doing? And if they figured out what I was doing, would they judge me? Every running road test beep declared that my son had a problem and the problem wasn't small, like biting his nails or getting cut from an athletic team or failing a college class. His problem was so complex that society dictated that he strap this tool on his car. I didn't know how much shame Matt felt. I didn't know if he could shed the humiliation or if it would drive him into deeper depression.

Again, my experience taught me that when individuals face the legal consequences of their actions, their whole family is affected. Our legal system does not allow for special treatment or leeway even when kind actions would benefit an individual.

Chapter twenty-three: More progress

The time Matt left home in a panic because he thought Steve and I were going to murder him, he later told me that he'd headed across Pennsylvania on Interstate 80 to Cleveland. In Cleveland, after a series of turns into a sketchy area of town, he became even more scared by figures who walked the sidewalks and streets. He headed home. He was gone for a couple days. I'm not sure where he spent his nights. Once he mentioned something about pulling the car to the side of the highway and heading off into the woods, where he sat on the ground or a log, for a long time, terrified that people were after him.

When he got home, we talked him into seeing a counselor who I found through a hotline provided by my work. We chose the counselor because we could get an appointment that day. (Since, I have learned that it's good practice to avoid counselors who can fit new clients in at a moment's notice. There's a reason that they have openings.)

This particular counselor listened to Matt's story of panic and terror. Then, I shared my story of bewilderment and fear. These weren't stories we'd tell just anyone. We told them because we thought that in return for our vulnerability, the counselor would offer help.

After Matt and I had both shared our hearts, the counselor rotated in his chair to face us both. He crossed his arms, so they rested on his protruding belly. He cleared his throat and said, "I'll tell you what you are going to do…"

It had been a long time since we had known what we

should do. I was so relieved to have found someone who knew what we should do. I took a deep breath. And glanced at Matt with a smile. A little bit of hope inflated my chest. Help is on the way, I thought.

The counselor tried to lock eyes with Matt and like I've mentioned Matt wasn't good with eye contact, so Matt shifted uneasily. The counselor declared, "You are going to give up alcohol for six weeks and if alcohol's not the problem, then that won't be a problem." His tone was such that he might as well have clapped his hands together twice and said, "That's that."

He pulled out his calendar and wrote Matt's name in two empty slots for the following week. "I'll see you on Thursday. No alcohol between now and then," he said.

The hope that had inflated in my chest collapsed. As we closed the door behind us, Matt whispered, "Mom, I'm not coming back here."

"I don't blame you," I said. Alcohol was a significant problem in Matt's life, but it seemed to me that an empathetic response that acknowledged our feelings before issuing an ultimatum would have helped.

With the ignition interlock device installed, Matt gave up alcohol. It seemed, he'd learned to value driving more than he valued alcohol. Even so, he was still locked inside himself, with no direction or purpose and oh, so, lonely.

And life went on. It was not ideal, but when Matt was working regularly, Steve's anger calmed, and it was easier to live at our house.

That year, the fall of 2012, Matt worked in grounds maintenance on a golf course. Around Thanksgiving, the golf course job finished for the year. And the boss told Matt to come by in the spring if he needed a job. This response was huge because it was the first time in a long time—maybe ever—that a job had run its course without Matt being fired from it. He had an invitation to return.

But he was still lonely and withdrawn. It was difficult to know what was going on inside his head. Not difficult. Impossible. Sometimes, I worried about Matt committing suicide. My sister said I should ask him.

"I can't ask him."

"Why not? It won't make him think: Oh, that's a good idea. You need to know if he is."

So I drummed up my courage and asked, "Do you ever think about committing suicide?" It took courage to ask because I feared his response. I didn't know where we'd get help if he said yes.

He said no.

Chapter twenty-four: Ski trip

A friend of mine owns a condo in a small town in Colorado. "You should use my condo sometime. Go visit Colorado. You like to ski. Take your family."

"Really?" Her generosity set me wondering if such a trip would be possible for us. Her offer made it financially feasible. The kids—all three of them—like downhill winter sports: skiing and snowboarding. I thought, what if we could travel as a family and enjoy a fun destination and remember the positives of being related to each other. What if Matt could reconnect with fun and be inspired to enjoy living again.

It's not like family vacations have always been all positive for us. But we have had some fun times together over the years that we remember fondly. The kids loved swimming and crabbing at Huntington Beach in South Carolina and jumping off the dock at high tide in the small town where my parents live in Connecticut. We enjoyed the Lake of the Woods in Canada where Matt who was just beginning to string sentences together (the first time we visited) was so excited to see seaplanes. "Planes on the pool!" he exclaimed. We've hiked and biked together. The kids weren't impressed with Niagara Falls. "This is it?" They found the Pittsburgh Science museum boring—their loss!

We made the plane reservations for the trip to Denver, Colorado. We mapped the driving route from Denver to the condo in Glenwood Springs. It wound through the Vail Pass. We began to talk about and imagine skiing in the Rocky

Mountains—something we'd never done.

We invited my sister and two of her daughters to go with us. Due to the timing of different school spring vacations, my sister, her daughters, Carolyn and I flew out a few days before Steve, Matt and Phillip.

Our flight to Denver was smooth and non-eventful. We stayed in a Denver hotel overnight, so we could drive our rented car during daylight through the mountains to Glenwood Springs. The ride was about 150 miles on Interstate 70. It's a good road, but we'd been warned that it can be treacherous in a snowstorm. "You might need studded tires. Or chains."

We didn't have to worry. The day was clear. The ground was bare. As we threaded through the towering mountains in the rented car on the road ribbon, we admired the angled rocks, the steep precipices and the clusters and long stretches of tall evergreens standing in ranks.

We planned to stop in Vail for lunch and arrive in Glenwood Springs in time to unpack before supper.

About an hour into our ride, dense fog rolled in and hid the vast mountain sharpness. Snowflakes swirled and obscured our vision. It was like a gray blanket had been draped over the car. In the light cast by the headlights, we could see tire tracks through snow on asphalt. My sister Colleen, who was driving, slowed, and in the outskirts of her vision, glimpsed the shadowy figure of a man on the side of the road. He rocked at the waist and waved his arms up and down in a vehement signal. Immediately, Colleen braked to a stop, almost kissing the rear bumper of a car in front of us which was stopped in the middle of the road. At a standstill, we took stock of the situation. We glimpsed the red lights— four glowing embers in a field of thick, white ash. We surmised that they belonged to two cars. One stopped in each lane of the road. In our mirrors, we could see the muted headlights of cars appear and stop inches from our bumper. I unrolled my window; the cold air invaded the car and the wet of blowing snowflakes bit at my face.

In a shouted conversation with a nearby driver, we learned reports of a collision ahead. We sat in the idling car, rummaging for snacks, wondering aloud about available restroom facilities. After an hour, the snow stopped, the fog lifted, revealing—three car lengths in front of us—a folded tractor trailer truck blocking the road and more than two dozen crunched and mangled cars in scattered disarray on the snow-covered highway, in the median and on the shoulders.

Weather conditions slowed the emergency personnel and clean-up crew's arrival. But eventually multiple ambulances came and left the scene. According to internet news, there were, amazingly, no fatalities.

In time, rescue workers cleared a path, so we could inch forward. We rolled past the pile of crunched metal and we headed on down the road. We'd been delayed, but not demolished or detoured. We were thankful to be able to continue our vacation.

The fog had dissipated, and we could see the countryside. We admired the rocks that rose on either side of the road. The evergreen trees dressed in new snow bobbed and curtsied in the wind. The vast and rugged wilderness seemed, to me, a showcase for infinity. We didn't talk. The car rolled forward. We gawked and felt our smallness.

After a bit, my sister said, "We've been driving for miles and I haven't seen another car in a long time."

I looked in front. I looked in back. No cars. We drove another mile in silence. No cars.

"Where did they all go?"

Maybe we held our breath.

"Do you think we are supposed to be driving here? Is this road closed?"

We sped along the road ribbon, rounded a corner, and drove down the hill near Vail. At the entrance to the Vail pass, on the other side of the road a large gate blocked the lane. A large, lighted sign read: Vail Pass Closed. Behind the sign, a long line of cars waited for the pass to open.

We didn't stop in Vail for lunch. We kept on, so we could get to Glenwood Springs by dark. We hoped we'd survived the worst the vacation would bring. (We were so wrong.)

We girls shared a couple of relaxing days. We talked, giggled and enjoyed remarkable skiing. At various ski resorts, we glided for miles down mountain trails with no one around. The roomy, outdoor expanse filled me with awe. We identified our favorite ski slopes, so we knew where to take Steve, Matt and Phillip when they arrived after a few days.

The morning of, but a couple hours before, their arrival, I went for a walk. From the front of the condo, I turned left. I followed a sidewalk uphill. The climb was almost as steep as climbing a flight of stairs. I walked slowly, but the uphill pitch called for exertion. I breathed heavy and felt a burn in my thighs. I stopped to rest and gaze around me at the mountains that towered on each side.

Our home in Pennsylvania is in a valley. It's like our town is in a bowl and the mountains all around rise to a crimped brim. I can look from most anywhere in the valley and in the not-too- distant distance, see a rounded mountain covered with hardwood trees that billow with green leaves. The mountains that surrounded Glenwood Springs were different. Their juts and angles shot up and loomed large, like they were leaning in—invading my personal space. They featured rock, not trees. At night their big shadows lurked. A constant, pressing presence.

As I walked, I wondered if Jesus meant mountains this large when he said that prayer prayed with faith the size of a mustard seed could move a mountain. On the walk, as I took in the mountains, I reminded God that I faced a problem, a challenge as large and unmovable as those rocky Colorado mountains. The challenge was Matt's depression; his failure to thrive.

"I think I have a mustard seed's worth of faith, God." I held my palm out in front of me and imagined a mustard seed—a little larger than a dot on a small i or the period at the end of this sentence.

"I don't feel like I have much faith, but if you could give me a grain of faith, I could pray and then you could move this mountain-like problem that is strangling our family. Remember years ago, when you let me believe that the Ephesians prayer for Matt had been answered? Please let this trip be a turning point. Step in and stop depression from erasing my son. Let him know your love. Make him strong in spirit."

With this prayer, I didn't hear God reply. I didn't even feel a glimmer of an answer, but sometimes faith means believing when the answer isn't evident. I turned around and started back down the mountainside, resisting forward momentum with every step.

I didn't know that in one short month I would recall the walk and my prayer by writing in my journal, "I prayed the trip would be a turning point, but I didn't mean a turning point to disaster."

Steve, Matt and Phillip arrived later that day. Fortunately, their trip through the Vail pass had not bordered on catastrophe like ours.

We spent days skiing. Everyone marveled at the scenery and the vastness of the snow playground. We all played, talked and joked, except Matt. He did okay. He went with us each day. He skied. Often, the kids would leave the lodge together to ski steeper and faster runs than Steve, Colleen and I skied. Invariably, Matt left with them, but quickly separated off to ski by himself.

One day, we got back to our designated meeting place at three-thirty in the afternoon. Slopes closed at five o'clock to make sure everyone was off by dark and Matt was missing. Fortunately, he answered his cell phone. He'd made a wrong turn on the mountain and the trail he followed led to another lodge.

All week, he was gruff and morose, but claimed to be enjoying himself. I strived to find a way to enjoy our awesome vacation without concern for Matt marring every minute. I couldn't let depression steal my vacation along with his, my life as well as his.

Chapter twenty-five: Panic story

For many years, when Steve and I discussed parenting Matt though anxiety and depression, our conversations became heated and often ended with us both on the verge of livid. However, one recent July evening, while we were on a walk, we talked in a cordial way.

It was a beautiful evening for a walk. The calendar said July, but the evening felt like June. Where we live in Central Pennsylvania, June evenings are perfect. The temperature cools. The sky turns brilliant blue. The clouds form intricate white lacy designs. On the horizon, the tall green trees meet the blue of the sky. The leaves of the hardwoods look like a kind of waving lace. The setting sun adds some pink and purple and blue hues to the sky. Dusk's soft light lasts long. Then the fireflies appear.

But the calendar said late July and a June evening in late July meant we must walk. On our walk through the beauty, Steve talked on and on about sink holes. As road superintendent of a local township, he had been interviewed on the six o'clock local news the day before. Topic: sink holes. And therefore, he seemed to think that the specifics of how sink holes form, the dangers they cause, and how to fix them made interesting conversation for a mile and a half of walking. But over the years, I have heard my fill of sink hole information. I have never seen a sink hole, but, from hearing Steve talk, I know enough about them that I could star in an hour-long talk show pontificating on sink holes.

"Could we please change the subject?" I asked.

"Sure." And Steve pointed to a crack in the road and began to talk about preventing cracks in the road and ditches and the road grades.

I listened as long as I could stand it. Then I said, "This may be interesting to you, but it's not to me. Could we talk about something that is interesting to both of us."

We praised the beauty of the evening and then Steve asked how my book was coming.

"I'm to the point where Colleen, the girls and I leave Colorado and you and the boys stay."

I wanted to hear his side of the story again. He didn't wait for me to ask. The words poured out.

This is the gist of what he said:

> So the morning you all left, Matt and Phillip and I went on a hike. Matt seemed pretty good. He joined in and, in fact, he and Phillip walked ahead on the way down. That night, we got a pizza and a movie.
>
> The next day, we couldn't get Matt out of bed to go skiing. "Matt, it's our last day," we coaxed.
>
> He responded groggily. "You go. I don't want to get up." And he rolled over and went back to sleep.
>
> Phillip and I went and enjoyed an awesome day. Although, I worried about Matt and wondered why he wouldn't get up on our last day of amazing skiing. He seemed okay when we got home. After supper, we went to bed, so we could get up early and pack before we headed home.
>
> In the night, I woke up to pee and as I walked past Matt's bed, I realized it was empty. I looked through the condo and couldn't find him. I went outside. He was nowhere around. I got in the car and drove through the streets of that little town looking for him. I couldn't find him.

I went back to the condo and tried to sleep. Of course, I couldn't sleep and as soon as the sunlight came in the window, I got up. I went to the front door. I was going to look for Matt again and there he was, pulling his rolling suitcase. He said that he'd been for a walk.

"Did you ask why he'd taken his suitcase on a walk?" I ask.

I was just so glad to see him back. I said, "Come on. Let's get this place cleaned up. We're going home today."

We cleaned the condo and locked it up. We headed toward Denver through the Vail Pass. I was driving, Phillip was in the front seat and Matt was in back. At one curve, we slowed down a little and, without warning, Matt opened the door and dove out. In the mirror, Phillip said he saw Matt, his arms extended in front, like he was in a dive, bumping down the road.

I pulled the car to a stop, put it in park and ran after Matt. By then he had run off the road into waist deep snow. We tried to talk him into coming back into the car. He resisted, so we began to pull his clothes off. We figured that if he got cold enough, he'd get back into the car.

Were there cars going by? I ask.

"Yeah, lots of cars," Steve says.

I wonder why no one stopped to see what was going on or to see if help was needed. Steve remembers luring Matt back into the car where they had him sit in front. They locked the door, and Phillip sat in back on high alert.

While driving, Steve called a doctor friend who thought that Matt must have high altitude disease. "Get him down to lower altitude right away."

They rolled into Denver, returned the rental car, and took the shuttle to the airport. At the airport, despite their coaxing him to calm down and stay, Matt attempted to run away again. Phillip tackled him and pinned him to the floor. They called for help. Security and medical personal came to assist. A medic sat with Matt and asked him if he wanted to get on the plane or to go to the hospital.

Matt chose the hospital.

I didn't think to ask Steve, but I don't know how they got to the hospital.

Steve told me that once they got to the emergency room, the administrative assistant who helped them with the paperwork, discovered that she and Steve were from the same hometown in Pennsylvania. In fact, she had dated one of his cousins.

"That was a God-thing," Steve said. "She really went out of her way to look out for us."

Steve called me from the hospital. I remember the call vividly. I had been home about twenty-four hours.

Like Steve always does, he delved right into the details. "We're in the emergency room. They gave Matt intravenous fluids and Valium."

"What?" He told me the story of driving through the Vail Pass, and I was so confused. What was Matt thinking?

"So you're leaving the hospital now?"

"I don't know where to go or what to do. Matt's a little calmed down, but he's still sort of panicked."

What to do? What to do? The most calming activity for Matt that I knew of was petting a dog. "Can you get him a dog to pet?" I said to fill a few moments while I thought.

And then I knew what to do. On our stop in Denver, my sister and I had connected over dinner with friends who we hadn't seen in years. This family had four young adult kids and they were familiar with some of the struggles young adults face. Over dinner, the woman had told me of being on a cellphone call with one of her kids and hearing the passenger exclaim three times, "Kevin! Kevin! Kevin!" before the call was lost. A few hours later, the police showed up at her door. Kevin and his passengers survived, but the vehicle didn't. And there were some drunk driving charges involved. For Kevin.

I felt a connection with this woman. I knew she would help, and I had her phone number handy as I'd added to my contacts just days before when we met for dinner.

The next message I got from Steve was a picture of Matt at a pet store holding a puppy. Carol had picked them up at the hospital and driven them right to a pet store.

I'm piecing the events together with bits from each person's story, so here's Matt's account of what happened next:

> After we missed our flight, we decided to stay in Denver for the night. We called some family friends who had moved from our hometown of State College to Denver a few years back. They said we could stay with them for a night. When we got there, it was nice to see familiar faces and I calmed down. The next day things went smoothly until my Dad, my brother, and I took a walk to see the sights of Denver. Panic set in again. I remember seeing the snow-covered Rocky Mountains in the distance and thinking about going back to a ski hill and going up to the top and proving to myself that I wasn't afraid to kill myself. Or that I wasn't scared of the pain of lying at the base of the back of a mountain with broken bones in the freezing cold never to see another human again. These were my thoughts.
>
> Also, I began to think my brother and Dad were going to try and kill me. I thought, I can outrun both my dad and brother. So I took a run for it. Well, I was wrong because my brother caught up to me and jumped on my back and tackled me from behind. After that they somehow got me back to our friend's house without me trying to run again. We had a peaceful lunch and then my panic sensors went off again. I thought that the people we

were staying with didn't like me and wanted to kill me. So I got up like I was going to the bathroom and bolted for the door. At this point I think my Dad and my brother were watching for me to try and run because as soon as I started for the door, my brother was up after me. I made it to the end of the driveway before he caught up and grabbed me and prevented me from running. I cried out, "Let me go! Let me go!"

Phillip shouted, "No, Matt, I will not let you go."

They got me on to the front porch where they duct taped my feet and arms together. Then we went to get the rental car that we were going to make the trip back in. I hopped into the rental car because they wouldn't untie me because they were afraid I would try and run away again.

We set off for State College. I was in back and slept for half the way back. I think I woke up and we were in Indiana. I said, "I have to pee."

So, we pulled over. "Do you still want to run," they asked before they released me.

"No," I said, but really, I had a thought to run out into the field in front of where I was peeing and just never look back.

Chapter twenty-six: Chaos

When I learned that, due to Matt's bizarre mental state, Steve, Matt and Phillip were driving all the way home, 1,555.4 miles, about twenty-three hours of driving, I started to pray. And I didn't know when I should stop. Should I stay up all night and pray?

I called a friend who has agonized over some of life's challenges, and she said that she thinks that sometimes it's a sign of faith to mention something to God and leave it with him. "You should probably get as much sleep as you can. They're going to be tired when they get home and Matt might need you."

I laid my head on the pillow and, to my surprise, slept soundly. I felt a little guilty about that when I woke in the morning and called Steve. They had driven all night. Matt was still in the car.

It was about five o'clock that afternoon when I heard the crunch of their tires on the driveway.

The plan was that once they came in and got settled, my sister and I would take their rental car to the Harrisburg airport (ninety-seven miles) where they'd left our car in extended parking.

Matt came in the back door. The dog greeted him joyfully. He reached down to pet the dog with both hands. I stooped to hug Matt's shoulders. "How are you?" I asked.

"Not real good," he said and shifted his gaze away from mine.

"You're home. That's good."

He seemed to agree. A moment later, I saw him furtively take a mini-survival kit from a cupboard near the door.

"What's that?" I asked.

"This?" He said too nonchalantly, holding up the mini-survival kit. "This came with my ski jacket." He had purchased a ski jacket for the trip. He slipped the survival kit into the pocket of his ski jacket which he was wearing.

"Are you thinking of leaving now?" My words trailed after him as he bolted out the door.

I hollered for help. Phillip and Steve ran after him, caught him and herded him into the living room insisting, "Matt, you can't run!"

"I'm going to wrap this duct tape around your legs again." Steve pulled out the roll of tape. "You can't run. We have to figure out what to do."

Matt sat in the living room on the couch, willingly, and Steve and Phillip wrapped his legs together in duct tape. We all sat down. I sat next to Matt. He took off his jacket and I rubbed his back. And I suppose we could have sat there indefinitely. At that moment, he was physically safe.

But we felt compelled by urgency. We had to do something. I got the phone book and paged through it. I found the number of a crisis hotline and called it. They said they'd dispatch a crisis counselor to our house.

My sister texted, "Are you ready to go to the airport?"

I texted, "No. I don't think I can go now."

She texted, "Should I come over?"

I texted, "Yes."

The crisis counselor arrived and said that she needed to ask Matt a few questions. I don't recall the questions she asked. For a while, I sat next to Matt on the couch, rubbing his back, studying the red blotches on the counselor's cheeks. The blotches kept getting redder and redder. I wondered if it was her first day at this work.

"You will have to take the duct tape off him. He has to go willingly," she said.

"Go where?" we asked. We were certain we would not take him to the institution he'd visited a few years back.

"The hospital."

"I want to go. But I want to brush my teeth before I go," Matt said.

Steve cut away the duct tape. Matt went to the bathroom to brush his teeth.

Steve went into the bedroom to pack a bag of essentials for Matt. I turned my attention to my sister and our plan to return the rental car. Phillip started to haul a suitcase to his room. The counselor sat in the living room.

All of us heard the front door slam. With only socks on his feet and no coat, Matt had run out into the cold. It was below freezing. Probably in the twenties.

"He's gone," someone hollered.

Steve and Phillip ran after him as quick as could be, but it was dark. Our neighborhood is illuminated by one or two faint streetlights. We live near a large wooded area. They could not spot him and did not know where to look.

The crisis counselor telephoned her boss and the police. The blotches on her cheeks and neck throbbed. Soon, her boss and a number of policemen—at least five—joined us. We have a small house and it seemed pretty full.

There was a quote posted on my refrigerator. It said, "Good morning. This is God. I will be handling all your problems today." I paused by the refrigerator door, read the quote, and reminded myself: God completes the tasks I can't complete. God passes the tests I can't pass. God does what I can't do. I kept walking to the refrigerator to read the soothing words again and again. There was a space in my soul in which I believed those words. But I worried, too.

A policeman, equipped with a clipboard and walkie-talkie sat at the kitchen table, manning the command station. He communicated with officers who scoured the nearby neighborhood and woods for Matt.

I thought of a very high highway overpass about three quarters of a mile from our house. It was at least the height of two two-story houses, maybe more. If Matt was considering suicide, and at that point, we didn't know about the thoughts he had, but if suicide was in his thinking, jumping off that bridge might occur to him.

I mentioned that to the police officer who was sitting at my kitchen table. He relayed it to one of the officers by walkie talkie, but not, I thought, with an appropriate amount of urgency.

I pulled Phillip aside. "Phil, I've been thinking about that bridge that crosses the valley down by Sellers Lane."

"I'm there," said Phillip as he went towards the door.

"Be careful. Don't get out of your car on the bridge unless—" He was gone.

That was okay. I didn't really want to put the unless into words.

I sat down at the kitchen table with my guests—a policeman, two crisis counselors and my sister. "Do you want something to drink?" I asked.

They all declined.

Maybe they were afraid to drink our water. Maybe they worried that the panic was in the water. Maybe there was protocol in place. Don't drink refreshments provided by the— what was I? The mother of the…? Culprit? The crazy?

Was I a mother who after all we'd been through would lose her beloved son to disaster that night? I got up and walked to the fridge. I read the quote. It reminded me that God had been through panic like this before. He would be calm for me when I couldn't. I don't know why I thought it was important to be calm. I guess I didn't want to stir up any more chaos.

I wondered if I should go look for Matt, too. They said they needed me to stay at the command post. In case they needed something from me. I thought fleetingly of mothers I had heard of who had to identify their deceased loved ones. I walked to the refrigerator again.

After a while, feeling so outside the realm of normal, I said something to the officer describing the circumstances as unusual. He said that the circumstances weren't outside the realm of usual for him.

"Really? You search for people in the night on a regular basis?"

"Often," he said.

"Do you usually find the person?"

"Oh, yes," he said.

Alive? I wondered. I was too afraid to ask. And I was glad this wasn't my usual life.

Steve fumed that three police cruisers with emergency lights flashing were parked in our driveway. "If Matt tried to come home, he'd be scared away. We need to move the cruisers."

I thought about Matt out there in the woods without shoes and without a jacket. Maybe he'd get so cold, he'd head home.

After a few hours, around ten o'clock, the officer got a call and when he hung up he announced, "The bloodhounds are coming." A search and rescue team from about forty-five minutes away was headed our way. I thought about my cousin who is on a search and rescue team and how she has said that many searches lead to a deceased victim, but that the find brings closure to the loved ones.

I didn't want that kind of closure. I wanted Matt. I thought, Matt loves dogs and dogs love him. I felt a surge of hope. I think they will find him alive. And finally, at command post, there was something for me to do. They needed some items of clothing that Matt had worn recently.

I found the clothing and then I thought about Carolyn and knew that I should call her. I didn't think she'd want to find out after the fact that bloodhounds were looking for her brother. I telephoned her. When I talked to her, she wanted to come immediately. She wanted me to pick her up. But I couldn't leave command post. She got her cousin Jackie out of bed and they started our way. It was about a fifteen-minute drive.

Before the fifteen minutes were up, while the bloodhounds still circled the house to catch Matt's scent, Carolyn, or maybe it was her cousin, called. "We have Matt. We'll take him to our place."

They had found him out behind a restaurant where he used to work. He was sitting by the dumpster, covered in layers of cardboard, trying to get warm. They didn't want us to tell the police where they were taking him, but we knew Matt needed professional, medical help.

Carolyn was distraught when the police arrived at her

place to take Matt to the hospital. She was angry with me. She was angry with the police officer.

I don't know if they handcuffed him. There are some parts of my own story that I don't want to know. I guess that's denial. My therapist agrees—its denial. But her kids are three and five. She can't imagine them in handcuffs.

The police took Matt to the emergency room of the local hospital and he was admitted to the behavioral health unit.

Chapter twenty-seven: Hospital

"Did you ever wonder if maybe Satan possessed him while he was in your womb?"

"Huh?" I wish I had been dreaming. A couple weeks after Matt was admitted to the hospital, a man approached me at church and asked me that question.

Two weeks into Matt's hospitalization, I didn't know what to think; many times, I wondered if we were fighting a spiritual or physical battle, but I sure didn't think that Satan had possessed him.

When Matt was a patient in the hospital, we met once or twice with the staff involved in his care. The hospital social worker hosted the meetings which took place in a very narrow room which was equipped with oddly arranged furniture. Maybe the small room was a former storage cupboard. We sat in chairs haphazardly scattered along the walls. The meetings never followed a defined agenda.

I'm a teacher. I like that my role is evident when I stand in front of the class. Unless I relinquish my place to a guest speaker or student presenter, that place is mine. I occupy it. I do life at that moment from a designated place. I establish an agenda and conduct the meeting according to the agenda.

In the hospital meeting room, I sat in a vinyl-covered chair that indicated nothing about my place. Steve perched on a chair near me. Down the room sat the social worker who was designated to help Matt transition home. He was a very large man and I worried that his chair was not large enough for him. To talk with him, I couldn't look at him naturally from my chair. I had to crane my neck. He was positioned to look straight ahead at a wall. And couldn't really turn to meet my gaze.

The hospital social worker sat in a chair position a way down from him and I couldn't see her to talk unless I scooted forward on my chair and swiveled.

I waited for someone to declare the purpose of the meeting. I wanted someone to be in charge. Who was in charge of the agenda? Who would conduct the meeting?

No one seemed to know.

Steve and I had taken off work to come to this meeting. And we had taken off a lot of work lately. Matt's wellbeing was way more important to us than work. But we had to tend to our jobs. We wanted to make good use of the time we took off. We wanted someone to conduct the meeting. We wanted someone to explain what was going on. No one stepped to the plate.

After some hemming and hawing, the hospital social worker determined that we should invite Matt to the meeting. Invited, Matt came in and sat down. He looked disheveled, sullen, and sad. He'd been in bed until he'd been invited to the meeting.

We sat in the room and chitchatted and waited for someone to get the meeting rolling.

Eventually, the large guy on the small chair said, "I'm the social worker who will help Matt transition from the hospital to home." I later learned his name was Mike.

Knowing that we'd have help transitioning Matt home felt awesome. I didn't know we'd have help doing that.

"So when will that transition take place?" I asked. Or, maybe, Steve asked.

"We don't know. The psychiatrist dictates that and…Matt have you talked to the psychiatrist today?"

"Nope. Not yet. Is that it? I'd like to go back to my room." Matt squirmed sitting in the narrow room, at the meeting with no agenda and I did, too. But Matt had said more words in a row than I'd heard him say in a long time. I felt kind of thankful. And he knew what he wanted to do. He had a desire, a preference.

The hospital social worker said Matt could go. And he left. But before he left, he looked at Steve and I questioning. And we said, "We'll come to your room when the meeting is over."

The hospital social worker said, "See he's not ready to go home yet. He's uncomfortable sitting in this meeting," and then she followed Matt out.

I wondered if I told her how antsy I felt in the meeting if they would keep me in the hospital, too. And sometimes, I thought that staying in a place where I had a clean bed and ample food and people looking in on me now and then would feel good. I'd feel cocooned in safety, I think. There'd be few decisions to be made. No papers to grade. No figuring out how to get to the grocery store or smiling at co-workers or students who didn't know anything was amiss in my life. No trying to keep students learning about commas or word choice.

But back to the meeting. Steve and I made small talk with Mike the social worker who said he was looking forward to helping Matt transition. He stated that there were a couple of options for Matt after the hospital. One was a day treatment place where he could go and be with others who'd been in the same position as he. The county would pay for a couple days a week. And it would be up to Matt. But we could tour the place when Matt got out and Matt could decide if he wanted to transition there.

I had never heard of such a place, and lately, Matt had not been much of a joiner, but, I thought, there was no harm in touring such a place.

The hospital social worker came back into the room. She said, "I ran into the psychiatrist while I was in the hall. She wants to meet with Matt. I told him that and he said that he was going to have a shower first." She shrugged. "That just shows that he's not thinking clearly."

In my mind, I disagreed with that conclusion. I could imagine Matt thinking that getting a shower before meeting with the psychiatrist was appropriate.

While Matt was showering, the psychiatrist came in the

narrow room to meet with us. I think she was the first psychiatrist I'd ever seen that was not in the movie "Killing of the Lambs" or "One Flew Over the Cuckoo's Nest." She was dressed in corduroy pants and a t-shirt type top. Her long, wavy, auburn hair hung over her back to her waist. She was skinny. And she wore clogs. She said that Matt's diagnosis was anxiety and depression leading to a psychotic break and that they were trying different medications and…her voice trailed off.

I wanted her to say, "and he will be better soon." Or, "and he will go home tomorrow."

She said, "And he's not ready to go home today."

"How will we know when he's ready?" We couldn't get a clear idea on their thinking on the timing of event. One counselor said, "We just want to see him smile."

"He has a nice smile," I assured them. "I could bring in pictures." They didn't want to see past smiles. They wanted to see him smile now. The meeting ended.

Matt's sadness was plastered on his face and so deep. It was sadness with deep roots.

Sometimes when I visited, Matt asked when he was coming home. I explained that the psychiatrist was looking for some markers. And one of the markers was a smile. "They want to see you smile. Can you smile?"

He'd stretch his lips wide to show his teeth. The grimace wasn't a smile.

Another behavior they wanted was for Matt to participate in group therapy. Matt hated group therapy. Sometimes, he just couldn't sit there. He'd go to group and he'd try to participate, but then he'd get up and leave and then he'd conclude that the other patients, nurses and doctors didn't like him because he left.

I didn't understand why he left group therapy, but the nurses and counselors did. I assured Matt that they understood. But when a paranoid thought gipped him, there was no convincing him to consider another perspective.

One nurse mentioned another facet to consider before Matt came home, "We want to know the medication is working for him and right now it isn't."

I listed the criteria for myself and for Matt: smile, participate in group therapy and take the right medication willingly. Those are the tasks to complete so you can come home.

One day, the counselor who seemed to be in charge indicated that perhaps Matt would be coming home the next day. I prepared for his homecoming. I got colleagues to substitute in my classes. I purchased a carload of groceries. I prepared to latch myself to Matt and not let him out of my sight. We didn't know what he would do in an environment where he wasn't locked in and under supervision—would he run?

The next day, when I arrived at the hospital, the counselor met me in the hallway with a mournful look. "He's not going home today."

"He's not? Why?"

"He told the psychiatrist he's hearing voices again."

I felt angry. I wanted Matt to stop hearing voices. I felt fear. I worried that he'd never be healthy again. And, if he was hearing voices, there was part of me that thought he should have the sense not to let on. He was never going to get out. That was probably about day thirty of his stay. From my current vantage point, I don't know why I felt such urgency to get him out. He was so safe and cared for. I guess coming home meant his health was improving and I wanted health for him. I wanted a secure, good outcome. And I wanted it sooner, rather than later.

Also, I had heard rumblings that the hospital administration was thinking of sending Matt to a longer-term facility. The hospital in our town was a short-term facility. The idea of a longer-term facility scared me. It was a huge unknown. I didn't want them to determine to send him somewhere unknown and far away for long-term care.

That evening, I went to Matt's room. "Ready to walk?" I asked. Each day when I visited him, we walked laps in the hospital corridors. The pace wasn't strenuous, but the activity was a mild form of exercise.

We set off side-by-side. We walked past rooms with closed doors. We walked past rooms with open doors and sad people sprawled in beds. We passed one elderly lady in a wheelchair. "How are you tonight?" I asked.

"Terrible," she answered.

"Do you want to go around with us? I could push you."

"No. He has to walk with you. He's your son."

We walked a lap.

"Am I coming home?"

"No. You're not coming home. They said that you told the doctor that you were hearing voices this morning." I tried to not sound annoyed. And then I remembered an article that I'd recently read. It said that a lot of people hear voices. Merely hearing voices is not a concern. It's what the voices say that can cause concern.

So I gulped, mustered up courage, and asked Matt, "What do the voices say?"

"Different things."

"Like what?" I braced myself.

"Right now, they're saying: right foot. Left foot. Right foot. Left foot."

"You mean, as you walk?"

"Yeah. The voice is telling me how to walk."

"Well, if that's what they are saying, why can't you come home?"

"I don't know."

"Could it be that it's not voices, but your thoughts?"

"Maybe."

It sounded more like thoughts to me than voices. "Did the doctor ask you what the voices say?"

He shrugged.

"Next time she asks you if you hear voices, tell her what the voices are saying."

However, overall, Matt's behavior was still erratic. One evening he tried to escape from the hospital, by following a friend who had visited him out. The next day, he stayed in his bed and said, "I'm afraid to come home because Dad will make me get a job."

Matt didn't realize how much Steve's perspective had changed. We had all come to understand so much more about the diseases of major depression and anxiety disorder. We knew they weren't a choice.

Steve wrote out a paper and signed it. The paper said that Matt did not ever have to get a job again, or, at least until he wanted to. We agreed that Matt had one thing to do and that was get better. One thing he had to do to get better was take the right medication willingly.

Chapter twenty-eight: Pills

These days our dog, Echo (Ollie was hit by a car. Echo came after.) suffers from grass allergies. He rolls in the grass, which makes him itch. He scratches and scratches until the irritated patches on his skin get red and raw looking. The treatment that works is a medication for dogs called Apoquel. It costs more than a dollar a pill and sometimes, during severe allergy season, we force feed Echo two pills a day. It's a pretty pricey daily treatment. Good thing he doesn't have any other expensive daily habits. Good thing he doesn't drink Starbucks. I tell him: "Good thing you're an American dog. There are plenty of countries where families don't have two dollars to spend on food. If you lived there, easing your itch would be way outside the budget."

Echo does not readily swallow his pills. If we add a pill to his bowl of food, he devours every speck of food and leaves the pill. Sometimes, I coat the pill with peanut butter and Echo licks off every last bit of peanut butter and spits out the pill. I wrack my mind for ingenious ways to disguise the pills to get them into Echo, so his skin stops itching.

When Matt was in the behavioral health unit of the hospital, a regiment of pills was part of his treatment. In the beginning phases of treatment, the psychiatrist told us that chances were good that medication existed to help Matt recover. But she wasn't sure which medication. That's the thing, well one of the things with drugs that help people recover from psychotic breaks, the medication that aids recovery is discovered by trial and error and, of course, the medications have numerous, potential, undesirable side effects.

The patient must tolerate the trial and error and the patient must cope with the side effects. I had heard of medications for depression on television and the long scrolling list of possible side effects frightened me. Especially the side effect that says that the drug might increase a person's tendency to contemplate suicide. But Matt was in the hospital where he could be watched, so suicide was virtually impossible, at least the way he was trying, for the first few days, to commit it which was by banging his head on the walls and yelling.

We were nervous about the drugs and their possible side effects, and some people's tales made us nervous. Some people shared their stories of horror indiscriminately.

One person told us that his daughter had gone to the facility where Matt was placed, and the doctors drugged her all up and then released her and she was worse off than she was before she went.

Another person told us that his child had been in a similar place and gotten all drugged up and they took her home and got her off the drugs and got her weed to smoke every day. She was doing much better. Had we considered bringing Matt home and supplying him with weed?

However, our circumstances were that Matt was confined to the hospital until the doctor determined that he was healthy enough to leave and she believed a drug existed to help him.

The first drug they tried made Matt feel nauseous.

"You need to try it for a few days. Sometimes people's bodies get accustomed to the drug," a nurse said.

Matt refused. And so they tried another drug.

One of the drugs that Matt was on (Haldol) for a few days, to calm his psychosis, can cause uncontrolled twitches in people's necks. We weren't prepared for this side effect.

One evening when we went to visit Matt, like usual, we deposited all our stuff in the lockers, presented our gifts for him (a book and a pizza slice) for inspection, before we were allowed through the locked doors to the ward. After we were buzzed in, we walked down the hall and peered through a window into the common room where patients often sat on a couch and watched television.

Matt slumped on the couch. He gazed in the direction of the television, but his eyes were blank, his mouth flaccid, and, at intervals, he twitched. Alarmed, we pushed through the door. He recognized us, dimly. He seemed really distant. Like we were in a pond and there was murky water between us preventing us from the certainty that he could see or hear us. We weren't sure if he was aware of the twitching.

I wondered if he had taken one more giant step away from us. I wondered if our son was going to be forever taken from us, not physically, but emotionally and in thought and in ability to communicate.

Steve found a nurse and demanded in an urgent way to know what was going on. Why had our son regressed? It was his body, but we didn't recognize the affect or mannerisms.

She hadn't even noticed. To us, it seemed like life as we knew it was in peril. Like our now and our future were being reshaped to be drastically different than we'd ever imagined. To her the twitch was so by the way. "Oh, I hadn't noticed that. I can ask the doctor to prescribe a drug that will counteract that side effect."

Her oblivion and her nonchalance made us wonder what kind of a hospital our son was in. Maybe we should take him home and supply him with weed.

That day, it seemed to me that there was nothing right or good in the world that I could do as Matt's mother. Looking down the hallway of his life I saw institution. He would have to be watched and cared for. I wanted to stay and sit by his side. But he wanted to be alone in a space where he could stare at a television or lay in a bed and twitch. He repeatedly told us to leave.

Steve and I left the hospital and visited very dear friends who prayed with us. I was a shell, walking around, doing the things that people do, but fear had scrambled everything inside me.

The next day, we arrived at the hospital as soon as

visiting hours started, buzzed in, found Matt. The twitch had dissipated. The drug to curtail the side effects of the Haldol had started working. Matt seemed incrementally more alert and my fear subsided a little.

Matt took his medication with sporadic willingness. He'd take it a few times in a row and then he'd vehemently refuse.

The nurses adamantly persisted until he took the necessary meds while in the hospital. He was on ten medications. They were doled out morning and evening. I saw his roommate's medication schedule. It was doled out hourly and more than ten medications were on the list.

One evening a nurse met Steve and I in the hallway. She was a nurse Steve liked.

"She's forthright. She tells it like it is," he said.

I thought her severe manner lacked nurturing. She stopped us as we made our way to Matt's room. "If he doesn't take his medication regularly, it doesn't matter how soon he goes home, he'll be back in here. He'll be back in here." It was a dire announcement, I think. A declaration of this is how life is for people who face the challenge of mental illness.

But that evening, it sounded like a threat.

If Matt ever got out, I thought that I could make sure he took his medicine. I said so.

"How will you do that?" She threw up the challenge. I declined to mention the tricks I use to get the dog to swallow his pills.

"He's an adult. He needs to be responsible for taking his own meds." She said.

It was another nurse who helped me understand and determine my role in helping Matt recover—including how much to help him with his medication. She was the first person to acknowledge my terror, but she assured me that he would get well. She said, "Faith, his brain is broken. The part of him that makes good decisions is broken. Use that as your guideline for deciding how to care for him."

Her words welled up in me a determination that I would be present and responsible for Matt's care until his brain was well.

When Matt finally left the hospital, he was on a slew of medications. An anti-psychotic. A pill to combat the side effects of the anti-psychotic. Three anti-depressants. An anti-anxiety. Ten pills a day. Five in the morning. Five at night.

"I think he's on too many pills," Steve said. "We need to get him off these pills."

I could understand that feeling, but the nurse who had shared the broken brain guideline that made so much sense to me, also said that after twenty years of working in the behavioral health unit she knew that prayer and counseling and family support had impact—they were parts of the puzzle of healing—but the right medication was key. It would pull everything together.

Based on her confidence, I determined to follow the medication guidelines to the letter.

Like I've mentioned, I'm an A student. A students earn A's by understanding the pertinent guidelines and implementing all of them. The day Matt came home from the hospital, as soon as he fell asleep, I drove a mile to the closest pharmacy with his prescriptions. The pharmacist was able to fill all of them except two. Pointing to two lines on the prescription note, the pharmacist said, "I don't know anyone in town who carries these. You could try these other pharmacies." She showed me a list.

I didn't want to leave Matt alone too long. He'd been constantly supervised for forty-five days. Who knew what he'd do if he woke up and no one was home. Would he run? I calculated the time it would take to visit pharmacy after pharmacy. I looked at all the pill bottles on the shelves in that room. I felt embarrassed about the kind of medication I was getting. After I left, would they whisper in secret about a woman whose son was so mentally ill that she needed medication we don't even carry?

Tears started running down my face. "I'm sorry," I sobbed, embarrassed.

I explained our situation. The pharmacy manager picked up the phone and began calling. She called pharmacy after pharmacy until she found one about eight miles away that could half fill the prescription. And another one, closer who could fill the other prescription. "Also, I'll order some. If you need it next month, we'll have it in stock."

A passionate, tearful plea for help. Three pharmacies. Insurance questions. Paperwork. I don't know how a depressed person, without support, follows a medication regiment. Getting the prescriptions filled correctly takes alertness, dogged persistence and effort.

The pharmacist who helped me is a heroine to me. She didn't just dole out pills. She comforted me. She shared knowledge. She helped with insurance red tape. Weeks later, she recognized and intervened when the out-patient psychiatrist wrote Matt a prescription for the wrong drug.

Each week, I'd distribute Matt's pills into a container as large as a big book with compartments labelled by morning and night and the day of the week. Matt didn't like the large container. Looking at it made him feel sickly and weak, so I got a smaller one. Each day, morning and night, I'd hand him his pills and a drink of water. Often, without commenting, he tossed the pills in his mouth and followed them with a swallow of water. Sometimes, he'd politely refuse. I'd persist. I'd coax. I'd talk about the benefits until he took the pills.

A few times, he took the five pills from me, cupped them in his hand, thought a moment and hurled them across the room. That made Steve so angry. "Your mother is helping you. Stop that," he'd yell.

I picked up the pills and offered them to Matt again. I knew this whole situation wasn't easy for Matt. His brain backfiring in such a bizarre way made him feel afraid and angry. He felt perturbed over his stalled life. His mother bringing him pills twice a day irked him.

Only once or twice could I not get Matt to take the pills. Sometimes, I nagged. Sometimes, I just stated: you are taking these pills. I prayed. Always.

The pills made Matt tired and caused weight gain. He slept a lot. He gained weight. He felt sluggish. Sometimes, I said, "I understand why you don't want to take the pills. You won't have to take them forever."

After a few months, the doctor recommended that we cut the dosages. In psychiatry, determining how much to reduce them by is a trial-and-error process. As the dosage is reduced, I learned to cut pills in half and in quarters. I bought myself a nice little apparatus to use to cut the pills. It helped with precision.

By fall 2013, two of the prescriptions had been eliminated from Matt's regiment. He seemed to feel better. Less tired. No voices. No hallucinations. No obvious unclear thinking.

We were moving forward. To health. A few months later, a third medication was eliminated from Matt's regimen. Its role was to target anxiety. And he got off it too soon, we learned. But that's another chapter.

Matt began to take more and more responsibility for his own medication. When he needed a refill, he'd go pick it up. When Matt was going through the trial and error of finding the right medication and the periodic refusal to take them, a friend had said, based on his experience, "If they find the right medication, he'll take it." I could see evidence that he was right.

Once in a while, I still fill the pill boxes. Now and then, if I'm going that way, I stop in the pharmacy and pick up Matt's meds. Last time I stopped in, the pharmacist explained that one of the pills was going to be changed to the generic form. The generic form was less expensive.

"I hope the generic will work as well," I said.

"It should. But keep an eye on Matt's reaction and let me know if you have any concerns."

The next day, Steve and I were leaving for a Maine vacation. Matt was going to be home alone for a week. "I'll get your medications ready for you before I go," I said. The act was more for me than for Matt.

As I dropped the pills in their compartments, I gladly noted that there was enough medication so that the switch to generic would not have to happen until we got home. I wanted to be present to make sure the generic form worked.

When Steve and I got home from our trip, I noted that the pill compartments were empty, meaning Matt had taken them every day.

"You're really doing well at remembering your meds," I called to Matt. I was in the kitchen. He was sitting in the front room watching television.

I thought, I'll fill the compartments for next week. I mused that helping Matt become self-sufficient meant I should soon transfer the pill-doling task to Matt.

I opened the bottle of Wellbutrin and spilled seven pills into the cup of one hand. Then I used my fingers to deposit them one by one in the containers. Drop. Drop. Filling the container was easy for Matt was down to three pills once a day.

The bottle of Abilify was empty, so I opened a new pill bottle, noted that the pills looked unfamiliar and remembered the change to generic. I called to Matt, "These pills look different. They're the generic ones I told you about. They aren't blue like the old ones."

"Generic?"

"Yeah, remember, I told you about the switch. They substituted a generic for the Abilify. Those were the little blue ones. These replacements are big and white." I dropped one big, white pill in each compartment.

"What are they called?" I usually don't like hollering from one room to the next. He was watching the U.S. Open, I think. I reminded myself that it was good that he was engaging in his own health care even if it was from a distance. So I looked at the side of the pill bottle and called back, "I'm not sure how to say it. Apoquel. I think. I guess that's the generic replacement for Abilify."

"AHH, Mom," he called. "Apoquel is the dog's skin medication. I had to get him a refill while you and Dad were away."

Oops. I looked in the cupboard. Sure enough, the generic replacement was unopened in the cupboard. I quickly retrieved the large white pills from the pill container and replaced them with some little blue ones.

Matt had come a long way on the road to health. But I'm getting ahead of myself.

Chapter twenty-nine: Home

I want to talk about the hospital a bit more. In the hospital, bit by bit, Matt got a little better. His erratic behavior evened out. He half smiled when we poked our head in his door. He joined group therapy sessions and rated how he felt on a scale of one to five. He raved about the food. He took his medicine rather than throwing the pills across the room.

One time, he had company, some friends were visiting, and he made a joke. I can't recall the joke. But I remember the recognition I felt. His comment showed that the person I remembered him being was emerging.

Steve and I were invited to a meeting to plan Matt's discharge. There were plenty of people at the meeting. This time we were seated around a table. A lawyer was present. He scribbled a lot of notes.

They seemed to indicate that they were mulling two possibilities. One was discharge to home. One was moving to another facility, a long-term facility.

I was so confused. "Why doesn't he just come home?"

"Matt, do you want to go home?"

Matt seemed tentative. I feared that after forty-some days, he had become so accustomed to living in an institution that he didn't remember how good home could be.

"What if I run?"

Or maybe he didn't ask that. Maybe he wondered. Maybe I wondered. Maybe they wondered. Mental illness includes so many unknowns.

The experts around the table hemmed and hawed. I

finally said, "Look. My semester is over. I posted grades today. I have three months in which I'm not teaching and I'm willing to spend all of that—and more—looking out for Matt at home. Why don't we try having him home? If it doesn't work, can't he come back?"

"What do you think, Matt?"

Matt was tentative, but he seemed to agree that he could try coming home. I felt a little frustrated. How could he even consider staying confined here?

"I'm afraid that Dad will say that I have to get a job."

"Right away?" we asked.

Steve declared that Matt's health was our number one priority and Matt didn't have to get a job until he wanted to get a job.

Everyone around the table agreed to try. And someone said, "When will he be discharged?"

"Today?" I asked. I thought we should get out of there before someone changed their mind.

I can't really recall if he came that day or the day after. He had to sign a lot of papers. They handed me slips for a lot of prescriptions.

For forty-five days, Matt had worn flip-flops or slipper socks. He pulled on shoes, with laces, and tightened the laces.

We walked through the locked metal doors and out into the sun. "How does it feel to be outside?" He'd been in a building for forty-five days straight.

His response was neutral. Too neutral for my liking. I wanted him to throw his arms open and embrace being outside.

On the way home, we decided to get a sandwich. I pulled into the plaza that housed our favorite local sandwich shop. I parked in front of a beauty salon. A sign in the window said, "Walk-ins welcome." Matt ran his fingers through his hair. "I need a haircut."

"Now? I thought you wanted a sandwich."

"I do. But a want a haircut more. My hair grew a lot while I was in the hospital."

I didn't quite know what to do. I was preoccupied with

wondering whether or not he'd run. I thought that maybe I should go into the salon with him. But I didn't think me treating him like he was five would help him get better, so I decided to go buy sandwiches while he got his hair cut.

"I'll buy you a sandwich and then wait in the car." I said handing him some money for the haircut. I hurriedly purchased the sandwiches and ran back to the car which was parked with the salon in sight. But I couldn't see inside the salon's big glazed windows.

I sat in the car and ate my sandwich and wondered how the haircut was going. I thought Matt's show of independence was a good sign. It hadn't been too many weeks back that he'd been laying in a bed, too anxious to walk down the hospital hallway to group therapy. I was thankful to have him well enough to come home. I was nervous. What if he wasn't well enough? What if he ran?

I checked my watch. At least twenty minutes had gone by. How long does a haircut take?

I squinted and tried to peer into the shop. I couldn't see in. I wondered about going in and looking for Matt. "Hi, I'm looking for my son." I'd say when the receptionist asked why I was there. But I didn't want Matt to think that I judged him unable to fend for himself. I walked a line of when to let him fend and when to take over and do it for him. I needed to take care of him until his broken brain healed. How long does it take a brain to heal?

I glanced around at the surroundings. What if he took off? Where would he run? He was hungry. He wanted a sandwich. He had some money. Could he have ditched me? Should I go into the hair salon to see?

If he was running, then I should be looking for him. The sooner the better.

What if he'd gone into the salon, seized a pair scissors and now was running with a sharp implement for harming himself?

I need to go into the hair salon and find out, I thought. But that might not be good because me treating Matt like a child might diminish his confidence and God knows he was struggling to find that confidence.

So, I sat in the car and established a time limit. I said to myself, "If he doesn't come out in fifteen minutes, then I will go in."

I would go in on a pretense. I wasn't sure what that pretense would be. Maybe I'd decided to consider getting my hair cut or nails done.

However, I didn't have to manufacture a pretense because Matt came out and slid into the passenger's seat rubbing his hand over his newly cut hair, "How's it look?"

"It looks good," I said. "But what took so long?"

"There was someone in front of me. I had to wait."

I took a deep breath and promised myself that next time I had to wait, I wouldn't worry. Of course, some promises are impossible to keep.

We finished our errands and went home. Matt enjoyed seeing the dog and watching television on the big screen HD television in our living room. But he seemed restless—a little at loose ends. Like he didn't quite know what to do.

That evening, I sat on the couch to watch television with him. He laid down, placed his head in my lap and said, "Mom, rub my head."

I pressed hard with my fingertips and stroked his head trying to push the tension from his scalp. It was the first time in a long, long time that I knew he knew we were allies, not enemies.

I thought about life and parenting and how I'd never imagined how hard it could be. And how glad I was to have him there on the couch in my living room.

"I'm so glad you are home."

Chapter thirty: Haiti

A few days later, we toured the day treatment center with Mike the social worker and Paul the center's manager. The center was much smaller than I had imagined. It included a small gathering room, a kitchen, and a meagerly equipped workout room.

"What do clients do here?" I asked Paul. I was interested in knowing the initial, extravagant steps to get people's brains healing.

"We meet in the kitchen at about nine. We talk about the newspaper and do the Sudoku puzzle together. Then, a speaker might talk about a topic of interest like personal finance or how to budget. Clients will make a snack or meal together."

It sounded dull and boring to me. I was pretty sure that Matt would decide not to attend. To my surprise, he said wanted to go at least two or three times a week.

"Good," said Paul. "We have a van that can pick you up, if you need a ride."

"I think I'll be ready to drive soon," Matt said.

"If he's not, I can bring him." I was all for driving him and seeing him safely from home to safe place to home.

"If you can't drive and your mom can't bring you, I can arrange a van pick-up for you," Mike said. "You just need to let me know. You've got my cellphone number, right?"

He spoke to Matt. I didn't know if Matt had his number. I did. I could give it to Matt if he needed it. I didn't say that. Part of me was trying to let Matt manage this interaction.

Having established the ride strategy, Paul moved on to talk about start date.

"So, do you want to start next Monday?"

"No, I can't start then. We are leaving for Haiti on Saturday."

For months, our family had been planning a service trip to Haiti. Many of our extended family members were planning to go. While in the hospital, Matt had expressed apprehension about the trip. Steve and I had determined that it would be too much for Matt to go so early in his recovery. Steve had agreed to stay home with him.

"No, Matt, remember you decided that you didn't want to go to Haiti. Dad's staying home with you. Maybe you and Dad will go on a fishing trip."

The social worker said to Matt, "Going seems really important to you."

"Yes, I really want to go."

I waited for the social worker to explain to Matt why he couldn't.

"When do you get back? You can start here when you get back." Paul pulled out a calendar, Matt finished some paperwork, and I finagled to get the social worker alone.

"He can't go to Haiti." I began to explain the complicating factors: an airplane ride and Haiti is difficult on people who are in robust physical and mental health and we'd said Matt wasn't coming. My anxiety began to escalate.

"Clearly, he wants to go. The client making decisions for himself—that's part of the healing. I'll talk to his psychiatrist to make sure she's okay with it," Mike said.

Later that afternoon, the social worker reported that the psychiatrist had said Matt had been released with no restrictions. She thought the trip was a good idea. Clearly, she had never been to Haiti. Clearly, she had never tried to get someone on a plane, had them run off, and spend forty-five days in a hospital. And then leave the hospital and get on a plane the next week.

Clearly, Steve would not be in favor of this turn of events. Clearly, the organization wouldn't let us go. Clearly.

Less than a week later, with Steve and the organization

enthusiastically supporting Matt's participation in the trip, we'd stayed the night in a hotel room in New York City and were hastily packing our things to leave for the airport and our early morning flight to Port-au-Prince. (Our friends thought, rightfully, that the trip was risky. I knew allowing Matt to take the trip was rash. But friends were praying and as we traveled to New York, I felt an inexplicable peace that everything would be okay.)

It was five o'clock in the morning. The rest of the team waited in the hotel lobby for us.

After brushing his teeth, Matt came out of the bathroom, looking shaky. "I've decided I'm not going."

I had anticipated Matt's backing out at the last minute—maybe that's why I'd felt so peaceful. "That's okay. Dad or I will stay with you." I wondered who it would be. I didn't want to be driving from New York City to home alone with Matt in the car. What if he jumped and ran?

Steve didn't immediately volunteer to stay back. We both wanted Matt to be healthy and comfortable, and we both wanted to be on the trip to Haiti.

So I said to Matt, "Before we decide who will stay with you, let's try the deep breathing they taught you at the hospital to calm anxiety." I said a brief prayer and we started the breathing. About five deep breaths later, Matt said, "I want to go."

I figured that the trip through the airport might prompt additional anxiety for Matt. There was still a possibility that we might not end up on the plane, but I knew that when Matt was surrounded by team members who he enjoyed being with our chances of actually getting on the plane would increase.

Because Matt and Steve's travel arrangements had been so last minute, once we got to the airport and stowed the truck in long term parking, Steve had to separate from us and go to a different terminal. He was flying on a different airline. The rest of us got in line and one by one placed our passports on the passport scanner. We strategically placed Matt in line between Phil and me. I watched. Phillip scanned his passport and moved ahead in the line. Matt, check. Me, check. Carolyn was right behind me. She scanned her passport and a big red X flashed on the screen.

What?

In all the pre-trip confusion, no one had noticed that her passport had expired. Tears streamed down her face. "You are all going. I'm staying. I'll figure this out. Even if I have to get the truck out of long-term parking and drive to Washington. I'll get this fixed. I'll get there in a couple days," she insisted.

"Mom, you can't let her drive the truck in this city. Last time she drove the truck, she got the brake and gas pedal confused and almost drove into a creek," Matt stood at my shoulder and voiced concern for his sister.

My desire to care for each child—even though they were young adults—gripped me. My stomach sank as I wondered what to do. "Give me that passport. Let's scan it again."

The big red x blinked on the screen. Surely, I thought, if we could find a human and explain our situation, surely, any human on earth would let her through.

I thought maybe Matt and I should both stay with Carolyn, but she insisted in tears that she could find a friend to help her and that I should go with Matt to Haiti.

She pushed us on our way and before I knew it, Matt and I were through security and on the plane. Matt fretted about Carolyn. "Mom, I hope she won't drive the truck in the city."

"She won't," I said. I was pretty sure that she wouldn't even be able to get the truck out of the long-term parking. But I didn't know what she would do.

She phoned a friend who picked her up at the airport, gave her a place to stay, and drove her to the embassy Monday morning. She updated her passport and three days later, after lunch, I was sitting by the ocean in a white, plastic chair and I looked up and saw Carolyn's smiling face. That was for sure one of the best moments of my life.

It was difficult to leave her in New York City to fend for herself, but I've often thought that maybe Carolyn's distress was the distraction that Matt needed to make it onto the plane. In Haiti, surrounded by a team of people who looked out for him, Matt had an enjoyable and productive time.

Chapter thirty-one: Chocolate world?

When we returned home, Matt started attending the day treatment facility two or three days a week. He felt confident enough in his abilities that he drove himself every day. On one of the weekdays that he didn't go, his social worker came to our home to visit him. The social worker was a big guy. I mean really large. He had some health problems and was on medication for a number of different maladies. It seemed like an arduous labor for him to trudge from his van into our house. He'd come in and sink down into a chair. I was so grateful that he came. I always greeted him. I made sure Matt remembered the meeting and was ready for it. Then I left the room.

One day, I was in the kitchen making my lunch and I overheard their conversation. The social worker said, "I need to fill out this form, so I'll have to ask you some personal information."

"Sure," Matt said. At that time, Matt was agreeable, but still didn't talk much. He answered questions, but usually with few words.

"How tall are you?"

"Six one."

"How much do you weigh?"

"Two twenty." Matt paused, "How much do you weigh?"

There was a longer pause. I held my breath as I wondered how the social worker would answer. Would he ignore the question? Would he explain that he was the one asking questions, not answering them? Would he make up a number?

And why was Matt asking? Was he just curious? Was he displaying indirect resistance to the personal questions?

I forget the exact number, but I think that Mike the social worker replied that he weighed three fifty.

"Wow!" Matt said. He sounded like he was clearly impressed.

I snuck out the back door before I burst into giggles.

The social worker helped us immensely. He helped with paperwork, medications, and finding appropriate services. He set Matt up to be evaluated for social security disability. We explained that he didn't need it, since we would support him as long as necessary.

"He probably won't get it," he said. "But it's important that he's evaluated and that there's a record of the evaluation for the future."

Matt was evaluated and designated as capable of working in a stress-free environment. I was glad that Matt was evaluated as capable of work. I concluded the designation meant that he must be getting healthy.

The social worker scoffed at the evaluation. To him, it seemed an inadequate response to Matt's situation, "Like a stress-free work environment exists?"

It felt good to have someone on our side. I imagine he had seen plenty of people who needed social security help turned down. Clearly at that point, Matt could not have supported himself.

One day Matt came home from day treatment and said that he'd met a kid there who had recently been discharged from the hospital.

"That's awesome." I was so glad. He needed friends and maybe he and this kid could empathize with each other because of their similar experiences.

Mike, the social worker, was dubious. But I didn't pay much attention to his attitude. Sometimes I got tired of his reality checks. A friend is worth celebrating, I thought. But pretty soon the phone was ringing regularly. The caller identification revealed the kid's number and Matt would say, "Don't answer it. He probably wants me to drive him somewhere." I guess the other kid, let's call him Joe, didn't have a car or a license.

"Maybe you should answer it and tell him that you can't drive him." I really wanted Matt to become more assertive.

He declined. He said it was better not to answer. On the few occasions that Joe got through to Matt, he needed a ride somewhere. He especially wanted a ride to Hershey.

"He wants to go to Hershey? To Chocolate World?" It seemed a little odd that two young men, recovering from hospital stays in the mental health unit would go to Hershey Park together. "Do you want to do that?" I asked Matt.

He didn't.

One evening, Joe called a few times and badgered Matt into driving him to return some videos to someone.

When Matt came home from the outing, he came into the living room where I pretended to watch television, but really, the act of staring at the flickering image was my cover. Every time Matt left home, I waited, apprehensively, for Matt's safe return. He said, "I think I'm quitting day treatment."

"I thought you liked that place. And you love Paul. He's so helpful."

"Yeah, but I'm quitting. I think I'm done there." He sounded tentative. "I can't see Joe anymore." He sounded certain.

"You can block his phone number."

"I'll do that, but I don't want to see him, either."

I worried about what Matt would do all day without attending the facility. I didn't think he was ready to graduate from it. So, I called Paul, the manager. I explained that I thought Matt was quitting because he didn't want to see Joe and he felt pressure to give Joe rides and I didn't know why Matt couldn't just explain to Joe that he couldn't give him rides. I thought Paul could help Matt be more assertive.

Paul took another tack. He said Matt's concerns and proposed course of action seemed reasonable. He suggested that, as a next step, Matt find a counselor to see weekly. And then Paul said something that didn't seem to fit the conversation, "Matt is committed to getting better."

I felt like I'd nibbled on cookie and tasted a dill pickle. Or pulled on a shoe that turned out to be glasses. The words just didn't fit the circumstances. It seemed to me that if Matt was committed to getting better, he'd stick it out at day treatment.

He didn't.

One day, about two years after quitting day treatment to leave Joe behind Matt said to me, "Mom, did I ever tell you why I quit day treatment?"

This time I was watching a television show and had to disengage before I answered. I thought for a minute.

"Yeah. You wanted to get away from that kid who always wanted rides."

"But did I tell you why I wanted to get away from him?"

"So you wouldn't feel like you had to drive him places."

"That. But did I tell you what kind of places? That day that I took him for a ride? He took me to a dealer's house. We pulled up outside and he wanted me to wait in the car while he went in and returned his videos, but I knew what he was there for."

"A dealer? A dealer of what?"

Matt gave me a look that said do I really need to explain? "Weed and…other stuff," he mumbled.

It was in another conversation with Phillip that I became more aware of the potential catastrophic dimensions of the situation. Phillip happened to mention that Hershey is known as a place that people can go to obtain cocaine. And then it dawned on me. Joe hadn't wanted to ride roller coasters and sample chocolate. He was looking for a cocaine courier.

I was glad that Matt had found a way out of that circumstance. I was glad for Paul, the day treatment center manager, who must have been aware of the situation's dimensions. And I finally understood the social worker's skepticism.

What if Matt had driven Joe to Hershey and what if Joe had stocked up on whatever illegal drugs are available and stashed them in Matt's car and what if they had been stopped on the way home by cops? With the ignition interlock machine still on his car, Matt's claim of not being involved would have been implausible. We'd have been

mired in more legal complications and…
Excuse me while I extract myself from the "what if" mire.

Chapter thirty-two: Priorities

When I think back, I wonder if it was challenging to be my friend through all those years. Most the time, I was so numb. Matt's health was my foremost concern. Worry about him was my default. Still, I tried to function. I tried to have a life. I tried to be present for my other kids. I tried to be present for my friends. I tried to work competently. I tried to cover that I was always worrying about Matt.

Some of my friends say that they admired me. They said that they couldn't figure out how I slogged through. How I got up every morning. How I went to work every day.

So, as I once wanted to be, I was noticed, but at that point, I would have exchanged their admiration for Matt's health any day. Is there a place to go to complete exchanges like that?

On my insides I felt like roadkill, someone run over by life, but I developed some practices that helped me function.

I spent time fluffing up my mind. Like when a pillow is flat and you fluff it to reshape it. I spent time connecting with God by reading the bible and praying. I spent a lot of time practicing gratitude. I counted with gratitude God's new mercies each day. It took a lot of determination to focus on thankfulness. I felt so sad about Matt's state of being.

I regularly reminded myself of God's presence even though I didn't feel it or always see evidence of it. One time, during the years that Matt was so depressed, so in conflict with Steve that I thought my family would disintegrate, my sister and I went skiing for a day. After we'd completed a few runs, I rested on the edge of a trail and watched a skiing duo glide past me. The skiers were harnessed together in tandem and on the back of the rear skier a sign said: Blind Skier.

I could not imagine harnessing myself to someone and gliding over the snow-covered paths without eyesight. What an act of courage and trust.

For me, choosing a path down a snow-covered mountain includes looking down the hill, gauging the steepness of the terrain, (I pick out a path that's steep enough for a fun glide, but not so steep that I lose control of my speed), reading the condition of the snow, (I avoid icy spots and go toward powdery, but not too powdery), and assessing the presence and skill of other skiers and their ability to keep in their own space and stay out of my way. I like to ski in a wide girth. To trust someone to pick out my path with all the right criteria in mind? I would resist that.

If I skied behind someone else, I imagine that I'd hear the swish of other skiers behind and beside. When I'm skiing alone, that sound is an alert for me. I brace for those who might ski over the back of my skis, hitting my calves and causing me to boggle (it has happened more than once). I prepare for the impact of a snowboarder's body with potential to throw me into the unforgiving surface of the icy hill and leave my muscles aching for days. So to put all that caution into someone else's control? I would resist that.

As I watched that pair of skiers slide down the hill and marveled at the blind skier's trust, I felt God say, "Be the blind skier."

God said, "I'm the guide. I will pick out a way for you over the treacherous terrain, stick close to me and you will be okay."

After that, there were many days that I got through by whispering that phrase repeatedly, "Be the blind skier."

So there is surrender and there is learned helplessness and part of my task was to learn the difference. And to live surrendered, but not helpless. I have discovered that God does not step in and do for me what he has equipped me to do for myself. He's my guide. He goes before me and behind me to facilitate my passage to a place where I love him more.

Chapter thirty-three: God with us

In 2005, a soon-to-be graduating student, who as a freshman had taken a writing class that I'd taught, visited me in my on-campus office. It was during the same year that I prayed the Ephesians 3:17-20 prayer daily for months for Matt, "Give my son strength to live. Keep him company deep in his spirit. Overwhelm him with love."

The student told me that he'd come to Penn State as an enthusiastic Christian and was leaving without faith.

"I don't believe anymore," he said.

He knew Matt would be attending Penn State in the fall and he predicted that my son would lose his faith, too.

"I'm praying that he won't," I said.

"If prayer is all you got to protect him, you ain't got enough," the student said with conviction. The enemies, he said, were alcohol and parties and excess alcohol and knowledge and successful professors who don't believe and drugs. And lots and lots of alcohol. And questions that lead to doubt.

I hoped that he was wrong. I hoped and I believed with fluctuating degrees of faith that God would hear and answer my prayers.

As you've read, after this conversation, through the years of Matt's difficulties, it appeared the student had been right. My son Matt's first semester at college marked the beginning of a string of choices that led to disaster. He attempted and dropped out of college three times. Foolish choices and illegal actions meant a number of encounters with police, subsequent large fines, and legal fees. He seemed trapped in a cycle of anxiety, depression, and drinking problems that appeared unbreakable.

I never gave up praying or asking others to pray for him. I don't have a list of all the people who prayed for Matt, and for us, but requesting prayer became as common as breathing to me. I requested prayer in church, at bible study and whenever someone—friend or acquaintance—asked how he was doing. "If you are a praying person, would you please pray for my Matt?"

And people did. "I pray for your son every day on my bus ride to work," said one co-worker.

Another colleague shared her umbrella one day as we walked between campus buildings during a rainstorm. "Pray for my son?" I asked. We linked arms, and she assured me of her frequent prayers.

Over the years, people in Pennsylvania, New England, New York, Virginia, all over United States, Canada, Haiti, England, Spain, Jerusalem, and probably more, prayed for Matt and our family.

One day in the fall of 2013, about six months after his discharge from the hospital, Matt said, "Mom, I've got to go to bible study early tonight."

When Matt was unhealthy, there were days when he was so oblivious or confused, I had to tell him what day of the week it was.

When he was in the hospital, he had to work up the courage to attend group therapy.

Since leaving the hospital, Matt had been taking small, regular steps to health. He followed a regular schedule which included many healthy activities, one of which was attending a weekly Wednesday bible study with young men from our church.

I was so glad he knew—without me telling him—it was Wednesday.

"Help me make dinner and then you can eat before you go."

Matt and I stood in the kitchen side by side chopping

vegetables. Matt didn't talk a lot, but he was co-operating and willingly answering questions. I was so glad to work with him to accomplish a task.

We finished preparing dinner, and Matt ate quickly. Steve and I were still sitting at the table, eating, when, with his bible, notebook and keys in hand, Matt went out the front door. About two minutes later, with his bible in hand, he returned.

He leaned against the kitchen wall. "Did I tell you why I have to go to bible study early?" he asked.

We shook our heads to indicate that he hadn't.

"I'm leading tonight. That's why I have to go early."

A big quiet bulged in the room. This was the kid who six months before couldn't get out of bed to sit in a semi-circle with others in the hospital group therapy. Often, once he got there, overcome with anxiety, he'd abruptly leave the group and flee to his room. This was the kid who talked, but barely, in family conversations. We were still adjusting to the idea that he went willingly on his own to bible study.

I thought he might misread our stunned silence. I thought I should fill it. I used the first words that popped in my head. "That's awesome. What's your topic?" I hoped I wasn't putting him on the spot. I wondered if he knew his topic.

"It's a prayer from Ephesians. It's Ephesians 3:17-20. Do you want me to read it to you?"

I thought, I think I know that prayer. Word for word. By heart. But I couldn't speak.

"Yeah, read it to us," Steve said.

Matt opened his bible to a bookmarked page, and in a strong, clear voice read the prayer that I had prayed. Every day for seven months. Eight years prior. In 2005. The year that student sat in my office and said that prayer is not enough.

The Ephesians prayer ends with a sentence that says, "Now unto him who can do far more than we can ask or imagine." To me that statement inspires a lifting up, a surrender, an acknowledgement that I must do everything I can to help my loved one and I must trust Jesus who can do far more than I can ask with the outcome. That is the surrender that the experience of loving my son who grapples with mental illness taught me.

Could this prayer being the topic of his bible study have been by chance? It seems unlikely. I don't know how to calculate the statistical likelihood of the prayer that I had prayed desperately and repeatedly being the topic of the bible study that Matt happened to sign up to lead eight years later. And then I think that reducing this circumstance to statistics is like trying to eat a rainbow or hear sunshine speak. At that moment, as Matt read, I knew God was in that room, that he had designed that conversation, and the certainty silenced me.

I left the supper table in a daze. It was like the silence that had bulged in the room crawled inside me and…was that really the prayer I had prayed? Maybe I was mistaken.

I went upstairs to my home office. I knelt in front of the bottom shelf of my bookcase and I pulled out my journals from 2005. I paged to June. There, page after page, sometimes written in pen, sometimes scrawled in pencil, in as many different ways as I could word it: "God, overwhelm my son with your vast love. Make him strong in spirit. Let him feel your company deep in his soul."

I felt like I'd placed my head in God's lap and as he stroked my head, he said, I'm here. We're on the same team. I've got this.

For three days, I couldn't mention this story to anyone and then once I started sharing, I couldn't stop.

Chapter thirty-four: Thank you

Like I said in the beginning, I believe we lived the story, so we could tell. I have lived to learn that God is present and working even when it doesn't seem like it. Prayer, though I don't understand why or how, is key. I wish I could say that now I always pray with more confidence, with a greater sense of prayer's magnitude.

I learned healthy practices that I want to pass on. When you're living on the loving end of a mental health challenge: speak up. Escape that learned helplessness. Find a balance between actively seeking to make things better and surrender.

Help is available. Keep looking.

Helpers need to keep working to find ways to get the message out: help is available.

I see things differently now. I have learned to fear a little bit less. If I'm being honest, and I've tried to be with every word of this story, I still lie awake until Matt pulls into the driveway at night. Not exactly worrying but wanting to know that he's safely in bed before I fall asleep.

For most my life, interacting with others has included sizing myself up and comparing and contrasting myself with other people. I don't intend to do this. It just happens in an instant and without volition. Sometimes the comparisons are benign. I meet someone new and think: we both have blue eyes.

When I visit a classroom in Haiti and I meet a teacher, I think: We are both teachers. And by my standard—which is me—she is woefully underequipped. She has no access to books or teaching supplies.

I haven't set out to think this way. I just do. The practice can be destructive to relationships and community. I can compare myself to other parents, find myself lacking and try to eke out a way to become superior. I can compare my kids to others and try find a way for my kids to enjoy more. This is the comparing that leads to distance from others and to shame which destroys. And through our experience, I have said goodbye to this type of comparing forever.

We are the same in that we are broken people. We are people who are capable of choosing death instead of life. It is silly and wrong and sucks the life right out of us, but we do it.

Some people are different because they, like a woman I met when Matt was almost recovered, let the comparisons lead to acts of compassion. Let me tell you how I met her.

The brain takes a long time to heal. Almost a year after Matt had been in the hospital, he was working at a fast food restaurant as a cook. The job was not ideal for him because the food had to be delivered to the consumer with speed and as Matt said, "After you've been to Haiti, it is difficult to care whether a customer gets their food in under seven minutes." Also, the pressure to work fast, stressed Matt.

One day, an angry, drive-through customer snarled to the server, "It would be my pleasure to come in and shoot you all in your effing faces."

Police were called. They opened an investigation. The man was not identified, and Matt found the circumstances very disconcerting.

So disconcerting, that later that evening at bible study, he got out of his seat and asked two shady looking newcomers to leave. When they didn't, he punched them. In his paranoid panic, he thought he was protecting the bible study group.

At home, later that night, he told me what he'd done. I hoped, for the first time ever, that he was hallucinating.

We called Paul, the day treatment manager, for advice. He said matter-of-factly, "While unfortunate, for someone who's been through what Matt's been through, this is not unusual behavior."

The psychiatrist adjusted Matt's medication. Matt found an excellent counselor to talk to.

When he calmed down, he was remorseful and filled with regret and very afraid of the panic that could take over his brain.

The bible study leader took it in stride. He knew Matt's heart and understood a bit about mental illness. The pastor, the bible study leader's supervisor, was unraveled and determined that the act required a disciplinary response. Matt was barred from bible study for three months.

That hurt.

I said, "We can find you another bible study."

But Matt liked that bible study and he wanted to wait out the three months. While he did, I tried to spend time with him, so he wouldn't feel sad and lonely.

One snowy Sunday afternoon, Matt and I went to a nearby state park to go cross-country skiing. We were about a mile out on the trail and Matt wanted to take a route that was different than the one we'd originally planned to follow. I didn't want to—I thought the route was too long—so we separated, agreeing to meet at the car at dusk.

For a few strides, I enjoyed skiing and then began to wonder if it was too early in Matt's recovery to leave him to ski in the woods on his own. I began to worry. I calmed myself and skied to the car. I waited until dusk. I waited until thirty minutes after dusk. No Matt.

I tried to call home to alert Steve. No cell service.

I didn't want to drive from the parking lot to find a park ranger because I thought Matt would panic if he arrived in the parking lot and the car was gone.

The park seemed very empty.

Eventually, I saw a car rolling towards me on the snow-covered road. I ran into the road and flagged the car down.

I explained my situation to the man and woman in the car. I said that Matt and I were supposed to meet and that he hadn't returned. That he sometimes got panic attacks and I was really concerned.

The man and woman were about my age. The woman

compared herself to me. She said, "We have kids, too. We know how you feel." Her comparison ignited her compassion. "We won't go home until your son is found."

Her zeal made me think I should reveal that he wasn't exactly a young boy. Sheepishly, I said, "He's twenty-six years old."

I thought they might dismiss my concern and change their minds about helping to look for an adult.

However, the woman said, "That explains everything. We will look for him and we won't go home until you have your son back."

While I waited at the car in case he came, they skied with flashlights back into the woods until they found him. He had misread the map and taken a trail way into a distant part of the park. He was sweating and panicked and so glad to be safe.

I have learned that God hears and answers prayers, and I have learned to let my comparing prompt acts of compassion.

And our family has learned gratitude. One day, about a year after he got lost skiing, Matt came into the kitchen. Arms spread, he leaned heavily on the kitchen counter. "Where's Dad? I need to tell you both something."

My stomach sank. My heart started beating fast. I tried to read Matt's expression while I called for Steve.

When Steve came into the room, Matt cleared his throat.

I braced for bad news.

"The last few years haven't been easy, but you've been there for me through it all and," Matt paused, "I want to thank you. So, thank you." And he smiled.

****

But it's not the end...

So, this is a natural place to pause my story, but it's not the end of our family's struggle with mental illness. Families like ours, who face the challenge of loving someone who struggles with anxiety disorder, clinical depression or another kind of mental illness, discover that our loved ones can get better, but that return to health must be maintained and sometimes bouts of the illness return again and again.

This past year, Matt's depression returned with a vengeance and our struggle was daily and difficult. I often reminded myself of the tools I've acquired and mustered the courage to use them. I have mentioned them throughout our story, and I'll list them here:

1. Let go of expectations of a "normal" life. This idea doesn't mean your life will be "less-than" but it will veer from expectations and plans. And that's okay. Find ways to be grateful for the life you're living.

2. Share your struggles. Don't isolate yourself or clam up. Talk to your spouse. Talk to friends. Talk to a counselor. Find a support group.

3. Get professional help. Sometimes finding a counselor you connect with is a challenge. When I looked for a counselor, I asked two people I respected for a list of potential counselors. Then, I made a list of the counselors who were on both lists. I contacted the counselors who were on that list. I called three offices before I found a counselor who could fit me in without an extended wait. Fortunately, she was a good fit for me.

   Recently, Matt needed to find a new counselor. Again, I asked for recommendations and made a list. I sat with Matt and encouraged him as he called office after office to find an opening. Finding a counselor was about a three-week project. The waiting lists for some counselors were so long that they weren't adding to them.

4. Remember, mental illness is a disease. When a

person is gripped by mental illness, their brain is broken. That means the part of them that makes good decisions is broken. When you step in and demand actions (like calling a counselor), you may feel like you are interfering (especially if your loved one is an adult) but your loved one needs your help.

5. Remember that people with mental illness can get better. That's a reason to hope and, once the person is better, to step back so they can function as independently as they are able.

6. Medication helps. When Matt was first helped by medication, the type of medication and the dose was determined by trial and error. However, recently, Matt visited a new psychiatric professional who used a psychotropic test that used research to determine the type of medication that would be most helpful to him. The results were efficient and effective.

7. Say no to shame and stigma. Although, people are more informed and there is less silence about mental illness than there used to be, there are still times when shame and stigma are evident. Find ways to rise above it.

8. Churches are getting better at responding to mental illness, but there is room for responses to become more compassionate and complete.

Visit me at faithtmcdonald.com where I blog about the challenge of loving someone through mental illness. I welcome your insight and thoughts.